THE BIRTH OF JOY

PHILIPPIANS

DOUG SERVEN
BOBBY GRIFFITH

CONTENTS

THE BIRTH OF JOY

PHILIPPIANS

Doug Serven & Bobby Griffith

PRAISE FOR THE BIRTH OF JOY

Real, academic, and reliable research validates it every single time: people in the West, and especially the USA, are less and less happy. Despite the promises that everything is awesome, or soon will be awesome, we are increasingly disappointed, dissatisfied, and depressed. *The Birth of Joy* is a book that is very much needed today. Doug and Bobby's wisdom and insights are not superficial or trite. Each chapter helpfully explains the ancient wisdom of Philippians and provides valuable insight needed wisdom about how we can see and know greater, deeper, and more authentic joy birthed in our lives. As a pastor, *The Birth of Joy* is one of those books I pray that my congregation will read!

—Rev. Ewan Kennedy, pastor of Church of the Redeemer, Atlanta

I appreciate Doug and Bobby's approach to Philippians. *The Birth of Joy* is both accessible and still academic, both of which are important to me as a pastor. I spend a great deal of time immersed in academics, pastoral ministry, social commentary, Elvis Krewe parades, and various conspiracy theories. *The Birth of Joy* cuts through this and helps me focus on the Gospel of grace for not only my life but also for those around me.

—Rev. Ray Cannata, pastor of Redeemer New Orleans, and co-author of *Rooted: The Apostles' Creed*

ISBN-13: 978-0-9973984-4-1

This book is dedicated to those who have given us the most joy, our wives and kids.

Thank you Jennifer and Julie for your joyful, devoted, and patient love. You both have crazy husbands, but you handle us with grace.

Thank you to our kids for the joy you bring to our lives each and every day. We love you Sammy, Ruth, Cal, Drew, and Anna. May your lives be overflowing with the joy that Christ brings. May you never know a day without him. That has always been and still is our prayer.

ALSO BY WHITE BLACKBIRD BOOKS

ABOUT WHITE BLACKBIRD
BOOKS

White blackbirds are extremely rare, but they are real. They are blackbirds that have turned white over the years as their feathers have come in and out over and over again. They are a redemptive picture of something you would never expect to see but that has slowly come into existence over time.

There is plenty of hurt and brokenness in the world. There is the hopelessness that comes in the midst of lost jobs, lost health, lost homes, lost marriages, lost children, lost parents, lost dreams, loss.

But there also are many white blackbirds. There are healed marriages, children who come home, friends who are reconciled. There are hurts healed, children fostered and adopted, communities restored. Some would call these events entirely natural, but really they are unexpected miracles.

The books in this series are not commentaries, nor are they crammed with unique insights. Rather, they are a collage of biblical truth applied to current times and places. The authors share their poverty and trust the Lord to use their words to strengthen and encourage his people.

May this series help you in your quest to know Christ as he is found in the Gospel through the Scriptures. May you look for and even expect the rare white blackbirds of God's redemption through Christ in your midst. May you be thankful when you look down and see your feathers have turned. May you also rejoice when you see that others have been unexpectedly transformed by Jesus.

INTRODUCTION

In the 1950s, Chevrolet produced a memorable television commercial that called viewers to "see the USA in your Chevrolet." The ad agency invited the audience to a joyful experience, promising that if they bought this car, they would have the opportunity to cruise the highways and byways and enjoy the road.

In America, we are bombarded with messages that tell us joy is just around the corner. The average American sees more than five thousand logos and advertising images per day.[1] Every one of these messages tells us happiness is within our grasp. They tell us having more will give us the pleasure we seek, the delight we crave.

Instinctively, we know better. We consume only to find ourselves lacking. We fill our time with media, apps, relationships, independence, commerce, careers, retirement plans, sex, and more, only to find that we lack the permanent joy we seek. We resonate with Johnny Cash's haunting words in his song "Hurt," "And you could have it all. My empire of dirt." We find that joy disappears when we read the news or when we are in pain.

The ancient letter of Philippians invites us to joy—

today. The Apostle Paul wrote this short note to a colonized outpost in the Roman Empire, a city named Philippi. It was a mining city built to provide wealth to the Roman Empire and also where retired soldiers went to reminisce about their glory days. It was a city trying so hard to be like Rome that it mimicked its entertainment, politics, and culture. What's remarkable about this letter is that Paul was in jail when he wrote it, yet it's a thank you note full of joy. He calls the Christian community to rejoice in all things and to endure all things joyfully. However, it is not out of a naïve focus on dying and going to heaven, but rather out of a willingness to embrace the reality of what it means to take hold of Jesus's life, death, and resurrection—to follow him in loving God and others.

Philippians invites us to joy and to find something in which to rejoice in the midst of our hectic, never-satisfied world. It shows us that Christ gives us himself and that through him we can find joy in chaos, poverty, and suffering. Joy does not have to be happy-clappy, pie-in-the-sky ignorance of the world we inhabit. It comes through viewing our reality in light of Christ.

We hope that through this short book you will come to understand that kind of joy. Jesus meets us where we are in our lives, not where we think we should be, or where we want to be. Philippians shows us that. It shows us the birth of true joy—found only in Jesus Christ.

DOUBLE RAINBOWS ALL THE WAY

PHILIPPIANS 1:1–18

I thank my God in all my remembrance of you, always in every prayer of mine for you all making my prayer with joy, because of your partnership in the Gospel from the first day until now.
—Philippians 1:3–5

What brings you joy? What is your ultimate happiness? What makes you absolutely giddy?

One example of exuberance that comes to my (Doug's) mind goes like this: "Double rainbow all the way!! So intense!! It's almost a triple rainbow!! What does it even mean?

Whooooooooooooaaaaaaaaaaa!!!

Double rainbow."[1]

As of September 2017, this YouTube video has had more than 44.5 million views. It's infectious. I'm sure that view total will grow more each year as it gets shared again and again.

We might be tempted to scoff at that video because we can often be jaded and cynical people. We might think Yosemitebear Mountain must have been on drugs. He says he wasn't. He says he was overcome with emotion at the sight of the double rainbows.

On the other hand, we're drawn to the video because it's so cheesy that it's also endearing. We're used to blunting our expressions and qualifying our opinions so we don't have to endure criticism if we're wrong. Not Yosemitebear. He lets it all out. Rainbows are awesome!

What is your double rainbow all the way?

Throughout this book we'll be talking about journeys and joy. We'll be looking at Paul's letter to the Philippians to guide us. It's an ancient text we'll use to see whether it has something to say to us, to see whether God's Word is relevant to us today. We believe Paul wrote this text, and that it is inspired by God. Therefore, Christians esteem it and want to put ourselves under its authority to learn from and commit ourselves to it. That's our goal in these White Blackbird Books—to teach the Bible in a way that connects with your heart and mind in a fresh way. We'll work through this book of the Bible section by section, drawing out principles and applications for us today. You may not agree with everything we say, and that's OK. You're invited to read and learn. Philippians is for all of us. It was written a long time ago to a specific people, and it also is for us today.

We'll get to know Paul better as we go along, so we won't go through his whole biography now. For the moment, we need to know that Paul has his good buddy, Timothy, with him, and they call themselves servants of Christ Jesus. Paul doesn't boast in his apostleship (which is an esteemed position), but he starts off with what will become the themes of this book—servanthood and joy. Paul is a leader, but he's also a servant under the orders and lordship of Jesus, his Messiah and Savior. And somehow, servanthood gives him joy.

What does Paul want us to know? Is it possible to find joy in being someone's servant?

Joy in the Saints

We can learn quite a bit from the introduction of any book. Though it is tempting to skip book introductions because we're in a hurry to get to the book itself, we really shouldn't if we want to know everything we can about the book. Introductions set the stage. They give us extra insight into the author and his or her intentions for writing the book.

Philippians begins in earnest in verse three, but there is important information to be gleaned from the two introductory verses. Paul says he is writing *"to all the saints in Christ Jesus who are at Philippi"* (Phil. 1:1).

What is a saint? When we hear someone say, "She's such a saint," what do we think of? Some of us grew up in a tradition in which people are inducted into saint-hood, a different category of person, someone who is much, much better than "normal" people.

And many of us hold the belief that Christians are supposed to be saints in a similar fashion, good people doing good things. We then get really disappointed when Christians utterly fail to live up to our idea of sainthood, which they inevitably will. We see Christians doing idiotic things all the time. They get in trouble. They cheat on their spouses. They lie and steal. They kill people. They hurt us, and they hurt the name of Christ.

Some of you don't want to have anything to do with the church or Christianity because of the ways you've been hurt by people in your church or your family. This is understandable, but it's not a correct understanding of the way Christian sainthood works.

The word "saint" does not mean a perfect person. The

Bible talks about how a saint is someone who has been chosen by God, who has been set apart by God, who has been loved by God with a special love. But saints aren't *better* people. They are just as messed up as the rest of us. Saints can certainly let us down as much as anyone, and they do all the time.

Saints lie. Saints cuss. Saints drink. Saints cheat. Saints kill. Saints hoard. Saints look at porn. Saints don't tip enough. Saints are racist. Saints tweet dumb things. Saints justify their actions to make themselves look good.

But that doesn't change the fact that saints are loved by God and set apart by him. They are still loved by Christ and forgiven by him. This love motivates them, albeit inconsistently, to live more God-pleasing lives. They're repentant in all the million ways they fall short of how they're called to live by God. They're thankful for God's grace.

In a sense, every person in the world is in the same boat. Everyone has trouble in our hearts and lives. Christianity doesn't prevent trouble. We all try to put on a good show. We work hard for our achievements (some of us work harder at this than others). We're proud of whatever we're into: our college careers, our parents, our church attendance, our virginity, our summer vacations, our voting record, our giving report, our ability to see through the crowd with cynicism and suspicion, our new diet, our neighborhood, or our ability to control our emotions.

Many of those things are good things. They give us a sense of identity and purpose. However, they're not the measure of our worth and can mask what it really going on inside us. Our hearts are way more confused, way more broken, way more questioning, way less stable, way less sure, way less confident, way less nice than we want to admit. Our hearts bear our hidden pains and sufferings.

What makes a Christian isn't how morally great a person is. None of us can be morally perfect. It's impossible.

Yet Paul says that *every* Christian in the church is a saint if he or she is united to Christ by faith. We're not saints because of the good things we've done, but because of the good things Christ Jesus has done on our behalf. Jesus is the one who makes saints. He's the one who loves and changes people. He forgives and loves people, even when they're not perfect, or even close to it.

There is a distinctive beauty to be found in such a ragtag bunch. Author Brennan Manning describes these followers of Christ as ragamuffins in his book, *The Ragamuffin Gospel*. With its negative connotations of disheveled uncleanliness, the word "ragamuffin" is arguably a more accurate descriptor than "saint." However, there is also an authentic Gospel joy to be found in the word "ragamuffin," a hope of something better, a taste of something genuine that we long for. It's a word that helps us be honest about the way grace works in our lives so we don't have to pretend we have it all together all the time. We don't! We're saints, and we're ragamuffins.

But it's difficult to walk along this Christian saint-ragamuffin path with each other. Sometimes I'd like to tell you that if you believe in Jesus, everything is going to be all right. I want to believe a narrative that says everything will fall into place for you with Jesus on your side. But I can't do that. I don't want to bait-and-switch you or Jesus-juke you. I don't want you to think being a Christian is the best thing since sliced bread. When you join the church, you join the dysfunctional saints in the world throughout time and space. There are crazy, crazy people counted as saints in the family of God, in the church!

So while I want you to be a part of a local church, I also want you to know what you're getting into when you start to march with the saints. People in the church are going to fail you. And you are going to fail them. But as we walk together with Jesus, in all our particular brokenness and frailty, there also can be great beauty and hope.

Joy in Grace and Peace

I know that's not a very encouraging picture. But right away you should know that by getting involved in a Christian community (the church), you are joining a collection of broken people, which is the way it should be. That's what the church is. It's the ragamuffin saints. We're saints because of what God has done for us. But what has he done for us?

In Paul's greeting, he mentions two key words: grace and peace. He writes, *"Grace to you and peace from God our Father and the Lord Jesus Christ"* (Phil. 1:2).

Philippians 1:2 states the real reason we are able to have any hope at all: grace and peace. Yes, we want to serve each other and promote strong relationships. We want to be actively involved in our cities. We want to go to the other nations of the world. We want to raise up leaders, elders, deacons, business owners, artists, politicians, teachers, and scientists with a biblical worldview and set them free to minister to our world. But we cannot achieve any of those worthy goals without the grace of Christ. It's all about grace. It hinges on grace. Grace is the thing.

Grace is God's undeserved favor, through Jesus, toward those who his deserve wrath. As Pastor Tim

Keller puts it, grace is the understanding that you are more broken, wicked, hateful, and weak than you have ever believed—yet you are more loved, cherished, forgiven, and cared for than you ever could have imagined. This grace is only possible and only true because of God's love for us in Christ. Christ took our brokenness and sin on himself and gave us hope and joy instead. He took the wrath we deserved and gave us life and a place in his family. That's the Christian message of hope and joy. It's the basis for all of Paul's writings.

Do you understand this grace? Do you know this joy of the love of Christ?

Maybe you don't. Maybe you never have or maybe it's grown cold for you over the years. Maybe you've drifted away. You started off excited, walked down an aisle, attended youth group every week, and went on retreats. But somewhere along the way, the lessons about Jesus became boring to you. Perhaps you got married and got busy. Or you became stressed by the demands of life. Or you were hurt one too many times.

Maybe you have a specific reason for being cool toward God and his people. Perhaps your parents divorced, and you can't figure out why God would do that. Or one of your friends died in a car accident. Or you've been persuaded by arguments saying the Bible isn't trustworthy and Jesus isn't who Christians claim he is.

But maybe, just maybe, there is something to this whole Christianity thing after all. Maybe Jesus is who he claims to be in the Scriptures, and even though the church is imperfect it is just the place for you after all.

If you don't know the love of Christ right now—whatever the reason—I urge you to keep asking God to reveal himself and his grace to you. Because God wants us to know just how loved and forgiven we are in Christ. In the

New Testament, Paul writes, *"God shows his love for us in that while we were still sinners, Christ died for us"* (Rom. 5:8) and *"There is therefore now no condemnation for those who are in Christ Jesus"* (Rom. 8:1). That's good news for us! There is grace for sinners through Christ.

Because of grace, we can have peace. It won't be perfect peace yet because we aren't in heaven. But we can have glimpses and tastes of it. You might experience a tiny slice of heaven when you're at the first football game of the year or when you're at the best concert you've ever attended. But even that beauty is just a taste of the peace we will have in the new heavens and the new earth someday, with the full restoration of everything as it should be, with Jesus reigning.

Until that time, we work for peace here, built on grace.

Peace means we're going to have to sometimes talk about difficult things and disagree and forgive each other and love. It means we're going to have to lay down our lives and fight for those who need an advocate. It means we have to reconcile and love our neighbors as ourselves. It means we examine our hearts and confess our sins and repent and believe. We'll have to hear others' confessions and forgive them, too.

Peace will take time. Peace will take work. Peace will take tears. Peace will come with love for all types of people. We need to walk with Jesus and allow him to bring down the barriers so we can have peace between Jew and Gentile, slave and free, rich and poor, black and white, good and bad, Republican and Democrat, committed and uncommitted. There is a peace that settles the soul.

Joy in Partnership

When was the last time you received a handwritten letter?

We don't get many real letters anymore. We get form letters, support letters, donation request letters, and bulk mail, but not personal handwritten letters. It's a lost art, a forgotten practice. But Paul didn't get to text or email. He had to sit down with the pen and paper, or pen and scroll. At least he didn't have to chisel his words into stone!

Paul's letter to the Philippians next describes the joy that comes from unity and partnership. He opens the letter in verses one and two by discussing the saints in Philippi, the overseers and deacons, and the whole church in the city. He mentions his sidekick and confidante, Timothy. He writes to the Philippians about all the things they're going to do together. He has those activities in mind because of all the things they already have done together.

When I imagine Paul writing this letter to the Philippians, I think he's irritated with them. He's spent his life traveling, and lately he's been in and out of prison. From other sources, we know that Paul has been confronted, attacked, and shipwrecked. I would think he'd write a harsh letter—Why is this happening to me?! Show me some love! Let's get some respect here!

But while Paul doesn't shy away from rebuking people in some of his other letters, he doesn't do so in this letter. Paul doesn't complain about his lot in life or his situation. This letter is a letter of joy, and he doesn't want to spoil that. We get the sense that the relationship between Paul and the Philippians is one of deep friendship. He loves them. He doesn't start off mad. He writes, *"I thank my God in all my remembrance of you, always in every prayer of mine for you all making my prayer with joy, because of your partnership in the Gospel from the first day until now"* (Phil. 1:3–5).

It isn't a form letter at all. It isn't an impersonal request. Paul's not asking for a donation to the Philippi Church Alumni Association. He is so thankful for them. He misses them. Every time he thinks of them and prays for them, he's filled with joy.

It's a deep sentiment that goes past just good vibes. There is a depth of relationship and friendship that is both intriguing and compelling. Paul says they have a partnership in the Gospel from the first day until now. He says they are *"partakers with me of grace"* (Phil. 1:7).

They're partners together. They're on the same team, sharing the same joy as they experience this grace, work, and mission together.

When I think of what Paul's words mean, three images come to mind. The first is the group of women with whom I spent the summer of 2010. My family and I spent the summer in Acapulco, Mexico, working with an orphanage. I had the honor of mentoring eight interns (who all happened to be women that summer). They worked with the kids, playing with them, teaching them, corralling them, and loving them. They also coordinated the ministries of the American teams who came each week to serve throughout the summer. The interns would facilitate the work projects, translate for the teams, and troubleshoot the crazy situations that would come up when team members got sick or injured or lost their passports.

I led a Bible study with the interns. We talked together. We prayed together. There was an intense but sweet partnership in the Gospel, as we took part together in the grace of serving in a foreign country. I'll never forget it. We did something important together.

There was joy in partnering together in Mexico that summer.

Another positive memory I have is sitting on my front porch with friends, during my time in Norman as a campus minister at the University of Oklahoma. When we sat on the porch, we didn't accomplish many tasks, but we did cultivate important friendships as we played board games or just sat and talked and laughed and cried together. I thank God when I remember those joyful times and those joyful friends.

The third image that comes to mind is the early days of starting City Pres, the church Bobby and I planted in Oklahoma City in 2011. I remember sitting with Bobby for hours in the coffee shop praying and dreaming and planning what our church might be like. I remember those first meetings in my living room with friends willing to show up and dream together. I think of our first worship services and those who helped. I think of the first CityGroups (small groups) and those who led and attended. I think of Brenden and the music team volunteering to do music and those first meetings when they learned six or seven new songs every week. I'm thankful for our first Stories of Rescue (personal stories of God's recent grace) and our first retreats and our first work days. I'm grateful for our first leadership team and first elders and all the amazing things that have happened as we've walked together and how great and hard it's been. What joy through partnership, even suffering together, wondering whether or not things would work out!

Paul has those types of pictures in mind as he pens this letter to the church at Philippi. He loves these Philippian people and their deep friendship and partnership. He has been through a great deal with them. He is so thankful for them. They're not partners with him just because they made donations or even because they prayed (though they did both of those). They're true, abiding friends, and thus, they're partakers in a deep joy together.

How can you find joy through unity? How can you find true partnership? Is it something you desire? Do you have friends who really know you and love you? Who are you getting porch time with and doing ministry with? Are you giving your life to something worthwhile, something greater than yourself, with the help and love of others around you? Do you show this type of partnership and support to others?

Another illustration of this type of joyful engagement is to imagine people dancing at a wedding reception. In this scenario, are you a dancer or a watcher? Are you in the middle or are you on the sidelines?

We understand that some people don't want to dance. They'd rather stand on the sidelines and just watch, refusing to enter in. I know why. I've been there, too. They feel awkward. They feel like everyone is watching them. Their moves aren't smooth, and their bodies lurch around awkwardly. They feel like they're ensuring a future without dating (even if they're already married and have nothing to lose!).

But they're wrong. This is the time to dance and go for it. It's the time to enter into a group of people who know them and love them. This isn't a dance contest. This is a wedding, which means people are celebrating, not evaluating.

People aren't going to laugh at them because they look silly or dance crazy—we all look silly and dance crazy. By getting over ourselves and joining in the dancing, we are partnering with and partaking in the joy of the couple, the joy of the wedding, and the joy of the whole celebration.

When we enter into authentic community, yes, we'll feel awkward. Yes, we'll feel funny. But there is a real joy in doing life together, and it's much more fun than sitting on the sidelines, watching everyone else. *That's* what makes someone an outsider. They're choosing to be an outsider because they're experiencing the party on the outside. They're evaluating instead of experiencing.

Be an insider. Partake in the wedding, in the couple's joy. It is fun to clear the dance floor to watch a really good dancer strut his or her stuff for a bit, but then we want to get back in there and dance with the rest of the idiots! And it is especially awesome when someone is willing to dance even when he or she isn't good at it. They show us there can be a joyful self-forgetfulness in joining in the celebrations of others.

We also appreciate listening to fantastic musicians and cringe when we hear ones not up to our standards. But... one of my favorite things is when there is a real freedom for those of us who aren't as talented to participate—in any area—in a safe setting.

For instance, I can't sing very well. You don't want me to sing solos at church. I know my limitations. But when we're all singing together, I'm going to sing as loud as I can for all I'm worth. And I can think of several people throughout the years who had bad voices (like me) but would sing in church as loudly as they could, with infectious gusto and passion. It was great!

I've also known people who didn't have great public speaking skills, but what they shared was great and benefited everyone present. At City Pres, that is what we call sharing our poverty. We don't only share our polished selves, but seek to engage and do things even in areas where we are weak. It is amazing what God can do with the weak things of the world.

We need this type of loving, playful, joyful participation in the church and in the world. We need everyone's gifts and talents, but we also just need everyone's participation, even in weak areas. The church is hamstrung when Christians only sit and watch and judge and refuse to participate. We need people to sing off-key and dance awkwardly. We need people to be willing to share their weaknesses, so we can rejoice together in Christ when there is even small growth inside or out. We need to partner together in self-forgetful joy!

Joy in Love

So you can see Paul's joy is more than a feeling. It's rooted in something deeper than temporary happiness from some cruise-ship, comfortable Vacationland. It's the joy of real relationship, deep friendship, and a partnership in task and vision.

Paul gives us more insight about this joy when he writes about love and service, describing what his prayer for the Philippians entails. Living with and walking with Jesus in the church and in the world is a full, rich experience.

Many have grown up thinking that being a Christian is just an intellectual assent, like signing on a dotted line. This approach to the Christian life is common where I live in Oklahoma. It's one of the ways people really get Christianity wrong. People think they can believe something in their heads without it touching their lives in any substantive way. People ask themselves, "Am I a Christian?" and then have a quick, ready answer, "Sure, I believe Jesus died for my sins." Except, they don't read the Bible, go to church, ask for forgiveness or forgive others, live lives of chastity or integrity or honesty or fidelity, or show mercy, or love people. Believing in Christ shouldn't create hating, judgmental people. It should make a difference in our lives, showing in love for God and others.

Another common way people miss the joy of being a Christian is they reduce Christianity to only being about living a moral life. They think being a Christian simply means "living right," without engaging in a real relationship with Jesus. Though they would generally never say it, these people live as though they have paid their dues to God by their lives of obedience and are "even," so to speak. They follow the rules. They're good people. They don't smoke or drink or dance or hang out with anyone who does anything like that.

They also don't hunger for God's grace because they don't think they need it very much. They may love that other people think they love Jesus, but what they really love is their reputation. They are missing the joy of knowing they are deeply loved, apart from their performance. Sadly, this type of person often requires a tumultuous fall from grace before she realizes she desperately needs a Savior just like all those "other people." This person needs to be confronted with how Jesus actually loves sinners. He came for the sick, not the healthy. He hangs out with the losers, not the righteous, powerful, good people.

So being a Christian isn't just about believing the right things or doing the right things. Ultimately, it is about love, both knowing we are loved and loving others. Love motivate us to know and serve another.

Paul's letter to the Philippians speaks to the joy that comes from love, not from intellectual assent or morality. Paul's affection for the Philippians goes beyond casual friendship. He says, *"For God is my witness, how I yearn for you all with the affection of Christ Jesus. And it is my prayer that your love may abound more and more, with knowledge and all discernment, so that you may approve what is excellent, and so be pure and blameless for the day of Christ"* (Phil. 1:8–10).

In this deep love, Paul says he yearns for them. The word "yearns" may seem an uncomfortable choice, but Paul talks here about intimacy without sexuality. He says he yearns for them with the affection of Christ Jesus, which is a powerful statement of love, of the love of the incarnation and perfect life, death, and resurrection of the Messiah. This affection isn't mere sentimentality or schmaltzy Valentine's Day card pithiness. It has depth and direction. He tells them what he wants. He prays their love would abound more and more and would grow deeper and higher and broader. He doesn't want it to just stay where it is. Paul helps us realize that our love for God and his people, for our friends and family, and for the world should be growing.

That amazing, compelling love is rich in content. It's not just a love that grows in some sort of nebulous blob of goodwill and happy feelings. Paul says love should grow in knowledge and depth of insight. There should be a continually expanding, winsomely held foundational knowledge of doctrine combined with biblical acuity and dexterity as we study and delve into the Scriptures and learn more about God's deep mercies to us.

This knowledge and depth of insight is something we often neglect. In other areas of life, we attend classes, read books, join discussion groups, and listen to podcasts so we can grow in our knowledge. Likewise, Paul says our love for God and others should grow, too. That's why it's good to read the Bible regularly, memorize Scripture and catechism questions, listen to sermons on Sundays and online, and pick up a good book to read and discuss with someone. There is always more to learn about God and his love!

Our love should grow in both knowledge and

discernment. As we understand the Scriptures more, we should be better equipped to discern and evaluate the world around us as well as our own hearts, but only in love. Discernment is love applied to knowledge. We can better see what we should think or do. As Paul explains, we can approve what is excellent, and we can be found pure and blameless in Christ because we stand in his purity and his blamelessness and his righteousness.

This means we have to stand for truth with each other, but we must stand for truth in love. As the popular Peter Scholtes hymn from the 1960s goes: "They will know we are Christians by our love." Not by our Christian t-shirts, car stickers, or social media posts. Certainly not by our messages of hate, judgment, and superiority. It has to be by our love, our truthful love as we stand up against evil, as we push back the darkness, and as we rejoice and revel in what is good.

What type of letter are you writing in your heart? Is it a letter of love or a letter of hate? What type of letter are you writing in the hearts of others?

I like the song, "The Ballad of Love and Hate" by the Avett Brothers. It is a beautiful, poignant picture of what we're talking about. In the song, Love and Hate personified write letters to each other. Love's letter says, "I can't wait to see you again." Love cares. Love forgives. Love pursues. It's powerful and persuasive. Love says, "I'm yours, and that's it, forever."

Hate writes a different letter. Its letter to Love says, "No one cares if you go or you stay. I barely even noticed you were away. I'll see you or I won't, whatever." "Whatever" is the ultimate dismissal. It makes a person feel small and lonely. Hate is rude, mean, and hurtful. It is known for what it is against rather than what it is for.

Love is different. Love pursues. We're called to love this way.

Joy in Service

A subcategory of both love and partnership is service. Love serves. The evidence of love is service, commitment, and sacrifice to another.

Paul has a deep, joyful hope for the Philippians and for us. He says, *"And I am sure of this, that he who began a good work in you will bring it to completion at the day of Jesus Christ"* (Phil. 1:6). This is a vision for hope in the future and also hope in the present. Those who are found in Christ, who are loved by Christ—the saints that Paul spoke of in his opening—will be brought to completion by God. Though it's difficult to fully grasp, being brought to completion somehow means one day we will be finally and ultimately made whole. The work will be done. The project will be completed. The house will be fully built. The race won. The goal accomplished. That won't happen until the last day, but it will happen!

This completion was never dependent on our good works, but on God's work in and through us in Jesus Christ. It is all of God, from beginning to end.

So when we speak of our love and our service, we shouldn't focus on ourselves, as internally logical as that might be. It's not our love and service. It's God's.

Earlier we discussed our knowledge, insight, purity, blamelessness, and righteousness. How are we coming on that list? If we're honest, we know those have been in short supply, and we as Christians need far more of those qualities. We need to be more Gospel-centered, truthful, merciful, and gracious. Cynics and skeptics have a right to judge Christians for not being known for their love.

But we also know that the acts of love we perform aren't even fully our own doing. Whatever our love, whatever our joy, and whatever our salvation—it is all from Christ. There is hope and joy in Christ! We can have hope in our future salvation and destiny because Jesus is at work, and he will finish his work, which is a comfort to us, and is where our joy ultimately rests. Paul teaches us this, and we need to grab hold of it.

Does your joy rest in something so sure as the work of Christ? Or are you resting in your own goodness or achievements? So much of what we take for joy is transitory or selfish. Let's take hold of something worth far more. Let's take hold of Christ!

When I imagine joy, my first thought is an image of myself kicking back at some all-inclusive resort with unlimited food and drink and massages, sitting under an umbrella by the beach with a book all day. Pretty shallow, I know. You might think of your performance at work or your kids or a new car.

None of those things are bad, but God offers so much more than just comfort or happiness based on circumstances. Joy in Christ is not situational. This is good, because those things will all either go away or lose their appeal. You will get bored at work. Your kids will disappoint you. Your car will break down. I will get sunburned on the beach.

Our joy is supposed to be found in something else.

Paul had so much joy and a Christ-loving perspective that he could see the good in any and every situation. In Philippians 1:12–18, he talks about how thankful he is for his jail time because he's had such an opportunity to see Jesus work in the lives of people. He mentions how others intended it for harm, but God worked it all out for good. God put Paul into that jail on purpose, and Paul realizes he should make the most of this opportunity. How many of us would see it that way?

If we thought like Paul—that God intended every situation for our good—we would seek to be content and make the most of even challenging situations. We would have joy even in the midst of disappointments, mistreatment, and weariness. That is not a typical response.

Paul says some preach Christ out of envy and rivalry. But no worries! It's all good. Paul is glad they're preaching Christ, whatever their motives. Paul pushes us toward a totally different approach to life.

Paul is pressing us to consider that serving isn't always on our terms and with our desired results. It doesn't look like we want it to look. It looks like what God wants it to look like. God will use us, and he'll even put us in trying situations and circumstances to use us.

If that's true and we can embrace it, our entire outlook will be changed. When I'm imprisoned, I can love Jesus. When I'm pregnant, I can love Jesus. When I'm single, I can love Jesus. When I'm in a nursing home, I can love Jesus. I can love Jesus really anywhere! So let's affirm where Christ is found, which is everywhere.

Paul writes, *"What then? Only that in every way, whether in pretense or in truth, Christ is proclaimed, and in that I rejoice"* (Phil. 1:18). Let's rejoice together! Let's rejoice in Christ and not in more laws, more rules, more morality, or more self-righteousness. Let's rejoice wherever and whenever Christ is found! The good news of the Gospel is that Christ saves sinners, and that is good news indeed!

Paul's type of joy is found in a serving and giving love. That is real joy.

It's not the vacation in the tropics that I want. It's much more substantial than those transitory things, and it involves giving away our lives. There is a true and deep joy in gracious, sacrificial giving. Christ's love is one of willing sacrifice, not of duty. It's the love that will not let us go. It's the love that chases us and finds us and will not give up. It's found in the death and sacrifice of Jesus that will stand the test of time, much more than our accomplishments or stuff. We're talking about eternity.

Dr. Bryan Chapell, former President of Covenant Theological Seminary, tells a story.

Years ago in my hometown two brothers decided to play in sand banks by the river. Because our town depends on the river for commerce, dredges regularly clear its channels of sand and deposit it in great mounds along the river's edge. Nothing is more fun for children than playing in these mountainous sand piles—and few things are more dangerous. While it is still wet, the dredges dump the sand on the shore from the river's bottom. As a result, the piles of sand dry with rigid crusts and often conceal cavernous internal voids formed by the escaping water. If a child climbs on a mound of sand where there is such a hidden void, the external surface easily collapses into the cavern. Sand from higher on the mound then rushes into the void, trapping the child in a sinkhole of loose sand. This is exactly what happened to the two brothers as they raced up one of the larger mounds.

When the boys did not return home at dinnertime, family and neighbors organized a search. When they found the younger brother, only his head and shoulders protruded from the mound. He was unconscious from the pressure of sand on his body. The searchers began digging frantically. When they had cleared the sand to his waist, he roused to consciousness. "Where is your brother?" the rescuers shouted. "I'm standing on his shoulders," replied the child.

With the sacrifice of his own life, the older brother lifted the younger to safety. So too did the One who is not ashamed to call himself our brother despite our waywardness (Hebr. 2:11). We live eternally by standing before God on the righteousness that Jesus Christ provided at the cost of his own life. This is the grace God extends to us and that we express to others as we use our every resource, gift, and prerogative for the good of another.[2]

That story is both tragic and amazing. What wondrous brotherly, sacrificial love is this! What joy to behold what it cost one to love another this way! It's the joy of the love that will not let us go. *"For even the Son of Man came not to be served but to serve, and to give his life as a ransom for many"* (Mark 10:45). True love requires sacrificial giving. Harry Potter has to die for the story to work, and in doing so he points to the Real Hero, Jesus.

Has God written this sort of joyful Philippian letter on your heart? It's not a letter written with invisible ink or on paper that will crumble and disintegrate. It's not a mean letter of hate to you. It's not a Dear John breakup letter. It's not a form letter. It's a personal invitation written for you.

It's the story of the Son of Man who came to love sinners. He came to live and die for us. Is this Philippian letter for you?

There is the quick joy of double rainbows. But even the ecstatic utterances of Yosemitebear don't last forever. Let's instead join the ragamuffin saints and discover for the first time or again the birth of joy, the kind that doesn't fade away because it is rooted in Christ.

2

THE ROLLER COASTER

PHILIPPIANS 1:19–30

For to me to live is Christ,
and to die is gain.
—Philippians. 1:21

Do you remember your first roller coaster experience? I (Doug) don't remember my first one, but I remember all four of my kids' first rides. When my youngest daughter, Anna, was eight, she rode her first roller coaster at Silver Dollar City (I love this place!) in Branson, Missouri. Their fastest ride was the Wildfire, which has a great initial drop and a few nice loops. It's not the biggest and best coaster I've ever ridden, but it's great, especially if there are no lines!

Since our extended family lives near there, we had been going to Silver Dollar City for years, but Anna could never ride because she didn't meet the height requirement. She had to watch and wait and grow. She'd see her sister and two brothers get off and go around again, and she'd be so sad.

But finally, at eight, she was tall enough. Yes! Eight

years old. After years of anticipation, she was finally standing in line. So excited. So nervous.

She made it to the front of the line for her first ride. She took her shoes off and put them in the cubby. She was strapped in. She'd never made it this far before, and things seemed pretty serious. But there was no turning back. She was resolute. She was stoic. Whatever was about to happen, she was going through with it. There's no real way to explain what it's going to feel like, is there? You have to experience a roller coaster for yourself. That's the only way.

We went up, up, up to the top. Then we had that feeling of weightlessness as we plunged to the ground. I still feel my stomach in my throat every time. But what was it like for Anna that first time she got to go?! How scary! But also what a thrill!

We're talking in Philippians about the thrilling birth of joy, which is found at the heart of the good news that Jesus Christ saves sinners. Philippians gives us Paul's thoughts on this joy and how it relates to our identity. There is a pathway of joy, a journey of much more significance than any short, one-minute trip on a roller coaster.

But like Anna's first trip on the Wildfire, our journeys through life often conjure fear and anticipation. Our paths are complicated, filled with suffering and joy. We get strapped in and then just have to hold on. Let's look at what we can learn from Paul about joy and our identity as we go on this Gospel ride.

City Identity

Paul talks about our identity, so we should too. Let's discuss identity in general and then apply it to where we live and how we act. We'll move from there into a deeper core of our identity, boring down into what really makes and shapes us.

What constitutes your identity? What forms, shapes, and changes our personal identity? We can talk about our IQ, our spot on the scale for our intelligence quotient (which is certainly a debatable measure).

We also can talk about our EQ, our emotional intelligence quotient.

We can discuss how our identity is shaped by our birth order and other factors from our family of origin, or what generation we're a part of, or what state we grew up in. We can talk about our gender identity, our racial identity, our cultural identity, or our theological identity.

Recently, I spoke with a mom whose son has struggled to find his place. She said he's always been shy and unwilling to fail at things. So he didn't try out for teams or try new experiences or have the normal ups and downs that people so often have. This accumulation of the way he is and the ways he's interacted with the world have come together to form him as a person. I suggested the son look into ways to grow his EQ and talked through an EQ book with him, which seemed to help. So people can change!

Paul hits some of these important identity markers in Philippians 1. Paul's journey of faith and joy is rooted first and foremost in the bedrock truth about who he is in Christ. It's not all about his IQ or EQ. He wants the Philippian church members to have their identity rooted in Christ. This identity has a directional or ministry component to it, which we'll discuss shortly.

Paul repeatedly calls people to move out in faith and joy based on their identity in Christ. He says, *"Only let your manner of life be worthy of the Gospel of Christ, so that whether I come and see you or am absent, I may hear of you that you are standing firm in one spirit, with one mind striving side by side for the faith of the Gospel, and not frightened in anything by your opponents"* (Phil. 1:27–28).

The Greek word translated as "manner of life" can also mean "citizen." It's where we get our word for "politics." Paul is saying we need to live a life worthy of the Gospel by being citizens who interact and participate with our world in the here and now. We are to live lives of cultural engagement. This is part of our identity as Christians.

It's easy and tempting to neglect this Gospel citizenship identity or get it wrong. One mistake we make is to establish communities without doors in or out. We can move into what people call the Christian ghetto. We can move into our own metaphorical or literal Christian gated community. We start to only do Christian activities, however we define those. We start to look for and shop exclusively at Christian stores or hire only Christian businesses to do our work. We only listen to Christian music and read Christian books, whatever those are. We only get Christian news, whatever that means. We make sure all our apps are Christian apps. Our time is spent doing only Christian things 24/7. Our attempts to live our lives this way can easily result in a strange, inescapable, echo-chamber subculture.

So one mistake is to pull back and stop interacting and engaging with the world. Another mistake is to think our job as Christians is to engage in politics and causes nonstop. We can use Christianity-laced, bombastic rhetoric. We can hand out (so-called) Christian voting guides and pressure everyone to think the way we do about every issue. While it is good that such people care about their cities, they can often leave a negative impression on the people they encounter. They can come across as self-righteous, judgmental, and mean. Their driving force can easily be fear rather than love.

It's important to care about what God cares about. It's good to look into what Christians have thought about an issue in a way that spans both time and cultures. We need to let God's Word and Spirit form our identity instead of popular culture or Christian subculture. We need to consider where we may have gotten something wrong. We need to consider what it truly means to love our neighbors as ourselves.

Both of these mistaken identities can result in extremely angry people. You know these people. Perhaps you are one of these people! We can lose our sense of delight and wonder. We trust less that God is in control or we opt out because we just can't take it anymore. We lose our joy.

Church shouldn't be our escape from the city and the world. In Philippians, Paul calls us to joyfully engage as vital, important members of our communities. He's calling us to an interactive identity. We aren't afraid of the city. We love the city. We engage in organizations, teams, projects, meetings, nonprofits, boards, task forces, groups, schools, neighborhoods, governments, and causes. Christians should seek justice and mercy. They should be advocates for those who don't have anyone to speak up for them. They should seek to change unfair, unjust laws or practices. They should seek to meet people and do something to make their cities better.

Engaged, city-identity Christians might even pick a place to visit in their city that they wouldn't normally go so they can be a part of seeing God transform that place over time. We shouldn't only pick places where we feel safe and untouched by the outside world. We can be a part of God's grace somewhere. We can be changed by others and experience the joy of togetherness instead of separateness. We can appreciate other cultures. We can celebrate the way individuals and groups of people are different.

Our identity as Christians should be that of a hopeful, joyful people who move out into and love our world. As Paul writes, we should aspire to live in a manner worthy of the Gospel, standing in one spirit, with one mind, striving side by side through our faith in the Gospel, not afraid. We stand together in the church, both humble and triumphant, going into the world with the powerful message of reconciliation to God in Jesus Christ.

But as we engage, we mustn't forget that our union with Christ also makes us a distinct people. We can love the world so much and its values and ideals that we don't ever take a critical view of it. We hold our Christianity in our back pockets, where it never significantly impacts our lives or challenges the values of the world. We can claim to be Christians, but no one could ever tell. Perhaps we are afraid to be marginalized and mistreated, so we never speak up for truth, justice, mercy, grace. Perhaps we just want to do what we want and get touchy if someone challenges our choices. But what does your faith change about how you live each day?

Paul says we're to *show* we are Christians. We're in this world, but we're not of this world. We're here to serve this world. Our ultimate citizenship is in heaven, but we're still citizens now in this place and time. What we do with our lives each day isn't what makes us Christians or saints, but real faith must come out somehow, some way.

We need to live our lives in a manner worthy of the Gospel of Christ. Faith in Christ should make a difference in how we think, act, feel, and relate to others. We can't just go on with business as usual. We can't just embrace all the idols of our culture and world and expect our faith to grow and mature.

How are you engaging your world? Are you an actively involved citizen who treats those of opposing views with dignity and respect? Are you serving the city? Are you loving the city? Or have you isolated yourself from your city and its people?

Does Christianity make any noticeable difference in your life? Could we look at your calendar or your debit card report or your apps and see that your faith affects how you live? Are you "living in a manner worthy of the Gospel" in the way you treat people, forgive others, date, marry, raise kids, and even determine where you will live?

As members of the Jesus-following, Gospel-believing church, let's move into town and become friends with people, loving them in a new and different way. It may be tough. You may get strange looks. People might not know what to do with you. But you also will grow in your faith and will be making yourself available to be used by God to bring redemption to areas of brokenness in your city.

Paul's citizenship was in heaven, but he also cared deeply for his people and his place. He wanted to live all his life for Christ. Can we say the same?

Church Identity

As we try to answer the call to bring the Gospel of hope to our communities, we cannot do it by ourselves. We need help. We need each other.

Paul says in Philippians 1:19, *"For I know that through your prayers and the help of the Spirit of Jesus Christ this will turn out for my deliverance."* Later, he says we are *"striving side by side for the faith of the Gospel"* (Phil. 1:27).

Paul pictures Christians working together as a team or a family. We're supposed to be the church, standing together, praying for each other, loving and helping each other.

My daughter Anna has played on volleyball teams. Six girls play at a time. They have to work together as a team to bump, set, and spike. They cannot win individually.

My son Drew rows. There are nine boys in the boat (eight rowers and one coxswain). One person can't row the big boat alone. They have to stroke together as a team, or they'll fail.

My son Cal played baseball in high school. There are nine players fielding each half inning. They can't win the game as lone rangers. Everyone has to do his job as members of the greater good, working together for the goals of the team.

My daughter Ruth works for a newspaper. She does her part and relies on others to do theirs to get the paper out each day. She can't produce the paper by herself. She has her beat, and she does her job. She also supports everyone else so they can produce the best product for the people.

There are individual sports and activities, but Christianity isn't one of them. We may train by ourselves, but we run the marathon together with many others. Christianity is a team endeavor.

So as you go into the city as a faithful, joyful citizen to reach your place and calling for Christ, you don't do it alone. Not only do you have Jesus, but you also have his church. You have other believers on the team.

It's easy for us to over individualize our faith. There is an individual aspect—each person must choose to acknowledge Christ as Lord and Savior—but once we are in Christ, we are part of a family. We join a group of people who are like us in some ways and not like us in others. We are called to love each other, even though that will be tremendously difficult at times. Yet this communal, familial aspect of faith in Christ is another place where joy can be found.

While our local churches are often too homogenous, the worldwide church is wonderfully diverse. It includes all personalities, backgrounds, nationalities, languages. Our collective identity is based on one true commonality, Jesus. He is what binds us together, allowing us to cut through personalities, classes, and races. At least that should be the case. If it is not, that is not the fault of Christianity, but of Christians. We're sinners and mess it up.

If you are a Christian, you need to join with others in this journey of joy, in this life of faith in and fidelity to Jesus. You are not alone. You're not singular. You're plural, so you need to join a church. You need to get help, talk to others, join a Bible study or small group, join with others somewhere somehow. You can't keep thinking you are on your own. As a Christian you are joined to the body of Christ. We need you to bring all your you-ness to the church. It's going to take effort because being on a team takes work. But we need to be for each other and celebrate the team and its accomplishments. We also need to support each other in our defeats and heartaches. We are in this together!

For an example of team togetherness, rewatch the movie *Rudy*. Remember, Rudy always wanted to play football at Notre Dame, but he stunk. He was too small and slow. However, he had tenacity and perseverance. He gave his all every play in every practice.

He had his doubts at times about whether all the work was worth it and almost quit a few times when he was never put into any games. Finally, before the last game his senior year, Rudy realized the coach wasn't planning to play him then either. The next day every single starting player came into the coach's office and offered to give up his spot for Rudy. Every player said he'd sit so Rudy could play. Every player said (in essence), "This guy is on my team. I love him. I am willing to sacrifice for him." So Rudy played. He didn't play much, but he did play, and his final success was the *team's* greatest joy.

That's unity. That's love. We step out together and say, "We're for Christ!" I am not just for myself, but for Christ, which means I'm for you if you're on my team. We are a community, called to love each other and stand together. Join in. Sign up. Come on. Let's stand together in love!

Ministry Identity

Paul has a city citizenship identity. Paul has a church community identity. And Paul also has a ministry calling identity. He wants people to know Jesus. He wants people to rest in Christ. This is another way he finds joy in his life.

The concept of a ministry identity forms the bulk of this section of Philippians. Paul writes, *"If I am to live in the flesh, that means fruitful labor for me. Yet which I shall choose I cannot tell. I am hard pressed between the two. My desire is to depart and be with Christ, for that is far better. But to remain in the flesh is more necessary on your account. Convinced of this, I know that I will remain and continue with you all, for your progress and joy in the faith, so that in me you may have ample cause to glory in Christ Jesus, because of my coming to you again"* (Phil. 1:22–26).

Paul longs to be with Jesus. He is tired of the hurt, the suffering, and the injustice. He desires to be freed from the pain and be with Jesus.

But at the same time, Paul is gripped with a minister-ial, sacrificial, Gospel-motivated calling. He has an identity in which he is an active member of his community. He lives in a manner worthy of Christ. He loves the church. And he is so moved by the Gospel that he wants to stay connected to the believers in Philippi with all his heart. Can you hear the anguish in his words? Can you hear the earnest desire?

Paul is saying he's willing to do anything to see people come to know Jesus as Lord and Savior.

Do you ever feel this way? Do you ever feel like you're ready for Jesus to come back or for him to take you to heaven so you can be done with this life? We were not made for this world and want to be in a place where we are welcomed and loved.

But most of us think "not yet." We want heaven, but not yet. We think we have so much to do. So our hesitation is not about Jesus and his plan. It's not because we want more and more people to know him. It's about *us*. This selfishness reveals a lack of a ministry identity.

Not for Paul. He was ready to see Jesus and honestly thought that would be better for him, but he didn't feel free to leave this world yet. Not because of his bucket list, but because he felt God wanted him to stay so he could minister to the Philippian church and contribute to their "progress and joy in the faith." Paul's passion was for Jesus and for others. To be with Christ was his desire, but he was willing to wait for their sakes.

His unselfish, joyful passion puts things in perspective, doesn't it? Are you in your neighborhood for others, or do you feel like your neighbors are there for you? Do you think your city is here to serve you, or have you been placed here in order to serve your city? Do you want to leave behind people who love Christ and his church when you're gone, or do you think people are here just to meet your needs?

We need to think about why we are on this earth,

why we exist, our calling. Sure we are meant to learn, work, serve, and enjoy life. But that's not all we're here for. Paul reminds us we are to live for others, to give our lives away, and to give up even the best in order to love others with the passionate love of Jesus. Paul is saying that a massive part of our Christian identity consists of praying for and working toward the goal that others would progress in joy in the faith and glory in Christ. This will often involve suffering. It certainly did for Paul.

We can start by praying for those around us. We can learn their names. We can open our apartment or house door now and then or go for a walk and greet the people we encounter. We might lead a Bible study or prayer group or fellowship meeting in our home. We might ask someone to lunch or coffee. We might invite someone to church or to a party. We might ask to pray for, help out, or just sit with someone in a time of need. We need to remember that people need to know Jesus.

We are called to reach this world for Christ. Since God has not taken any of us home to Jesus yet, let's serve and love others while we're here, asking God to make our passion like Paul's.

Gospel Identity

Well, we're a little stuck then, aren't we? I don't know about you, but I'm not doing very well at these things. I am not pure and holy. I am not the best citizen. I'm not a perfect member of either a church or community.

I don't want to be in real, honest, authentic community (even though I say I do). If I'm being real, the real me throws people under the bus by ignoring them, hating them, using them, distancing myself from them. The real me doesn't want to visit them in the hospital, and thinks they're crazy for disagreeing with me. The real me talks bad about them behind their backs. And I'm a pastor!

Can I just start to do better? Am I supposed to pull myself up by my bootstraps and fix all those things? Sometimes I feel willing to make a go at it, so that other people or my wife or my kids will like me better. Other times, the task seems so overwhelming that I don't even want to try. It's better to throw in the towel, hope for the best, hope for forgiveness, and just do what I want to do. Is there another way?

Yes. Two things can give us hope.

First, Paul says, *"For I know that through your prayers and the help of the Spirit of Jesus Christ this will turn out for my deliverance"* (Phil. 1:19).

Notice the end of the verse. Paul says that everything will turn out for his "deliverance." Paul isn't talking about getting out of jail. "Deliverance" here means "salvation." Translators are reluctant to translate it as "salvation" because they don't want to imply that everyone needs to be thrown into jail so they can be pardoned and go to heaven. But Paul is not saying everyone has to go to prison in order to be saved. We tend to think of salvation as only meaning the removal of the *penalty* of sin. That is part of it; it is the past tense use of salvation. Christians have been saved from the penalty of sin once we are in Christ. But there is also a present tense of salvation— being continually saved from the *power* of sin. When we are in Christ, we can have a freedom from sin's power. We don't always win, but sin doesn't fully or finally rule us any longer either. In the future tense of salvation, we can have freedom from sin's *presence*. There will be a time in the future when sin won't even be an issue!

Incredibly, the Gospel is for all of us, all the time! You may have been a Christian since you were a little kid or you may have become one as a teenager or adult. The

Gospel still applies to you and me and all of us. We all need the Gospel. We all need salvation. We all need deliverance in all of our circumstances, even now. That need for deliverance doesn't end when we become Christians. We trust God will use all our experiences and all our sufferings to bring us to salvation, to deliverance. We trust and hope he will bring us out of the penalty of sin, out of the power of sin, and someday out of the presence of sin.

Paul's Gospel identity is a message of hope and joy. We need deliverance. We need salvation. We need hope.

You may have wandered from the faith and are unsure today. The Gospel identity applies to you, too. Come back. Return to Christ.

You need the Gospel today. It should never get old to you. You don't ever move past it on to something else. Yes, there is work to be done in this world. But there is also freedom and rest in Christ because he has done the work and paid the price and set us free from the bondage of sin. The Gospel is for you today. May you embrace Christ and love him and know his deep, deep love for you, which is not dependent on your work. May that joy capture your heart.

May you say along with Paul, *"For to me to live is Christ, and to die is gain"* (Phil. 1:21).

That's the key. To live is Christ.

Can you say that? If not, what's your alternative? For to me to live is _____. What goes your blank? For to me to live is success? Power? Pleasure? Security? Marriage? Some peace and quiet? Relief from suffering? There is something in your blank, something you live for. Think about what you crave, what you believe will make you happy.

There also are things you wanted, but after you got them they didn't satisfy so you moved on to something else. Do you remember badly wanting your driver's license? But now it doesn't seem so exciting. Do you remember when you wanted a new phone? Now you've had that phone for awhile, and it stinks in comparison to the latest model.

I remember when I simply wanted a TV that worked. Now I want HD. I remember when for me to live was to have a book listed on Amazon. I remember when I said many times how great it would be to be married and have kids. I remember when I wanted to have a church of one hundred, two hundred, three hundred people. Now I want more. The thing in the blank keeps changing!

The blank you're living for might be potty-trained kids. It may be to be in high school or college. It may be to make $30,000 a year or $100k or $1 million. It might be to control your own schedule. It could be anything. Whatever it is—that's your bottom line.

Paul's bottom line was Jesus. He lived for Christ, and Christ was big enough, strong enough, and forgiving enough that Paul could make it through anything. Because Paul was so connected to Christ, he didn't stand up and say, "I am Paul!" He stood up and said, "I am Christ's." He wanted to stay in this world and minister to others because he loved Christ and was captured by the vision of Christ in all his life. That was his ultimate identity. Everything else was secondary to that primary truth.

Can you say, "To live is Christ"? Is that your vision? Is that your hope? Is that your bottom line? Is that what you want for other people? Are you willing to give your life for that?

Let's return to Anna and the Wildfire roller coaster. When she rode it for the first time, she was brave but scared to death.

I, however, was not afraid. I was not worried one bit. I

looked forward to the thrill of the first drop—which is quite a doozy—but I wasn't scared.

Why not? Because I'd been there before. I knew the safety harness would work. I knew the workers would check and recheck the ride to make sure it was safe.

That doesn't mean the ride is no longer fun for me. But I get on it with confidence that it will see me through the quick journey, and I'll arrive back in the station ready to go again. There is a different kind of joy knowing the ride will be fun and I will be safe.

When the "life ride" we are on is not fun, we can still know Christ will see us safely through. It may be relational strife, parents' failing health, adult child wandering from the faith, or difficult job situation. Paul is telling us if we have our identity in Christ, we will make it.

3

JOURNEY OF JOY

PHILIPPIANS 2:1–11

*Have this mind among yourselves, which is yours in Christ
Jesus, who, though he was in the form of God, did not count
equality with God a thing to be grasped, but emptied himself,
by taking the form of a servant, being born in the likeness of
men. And being found in human form, he humbled himself by
becoming obedient to the point of death, even death on a cross.*
—Philippians 2:5–8

In the summer of 1993, I (Doug) made a journey of joy. I
drove from Springfield, Missouri, to Eagle Lake,
Colorado. I made the fourteen-hour trip by myself in one
day. I was in a hurry to get there. I didn't want to be late.
I had planned and prepared, but I didn't have much with
me—just one key item. I had a diamond ring in my
pocket, and I was afraid I would lose it. The ring wasn't
expensive, but since I didn't have much money it may as
well have been worth a million dollars. I must have
checked my pocket a thousand times to make sure it was
still there.

I spent the night at Eagle Lake Camp in Colorado
Springs, woke up very early the next morning, and hiked

a small but steep mountain as the sun rose. Then I hid behind a rock and waited.

Not long after, I heard voices. I was nervous. I thought my plan would work, but there was still doubt in my mind. What if this didn't turn out the way I had planned?

But then Julie walked up, and I jumped out. My partner in crime, who had gotten her up there for me under false pretenses, left us alone. Julie was happy to discover that her suspicions regarding the strange morning hike were correct. I got down on one knee and asked her to marry me. She said yes!

Since the camp where Julie had been a counselor was finished for the summer, we loaded her gear and drove back to Missouri together, engaged. I'd bought her wedding magazines and a wedding planner, and the trip flew by. We were married six months later, marking the beginning of a journey we've been on ever since. That journey of joy took work and planning, but was worth it!

Philippians 2:1–11 speaks of the glorious attributes of Jesus Christ and also shows his journey of joy, which was to serve. This text shows us the route he took, and where his final destination is. Paul asks us whether we believe Jesus's path was for us. He asks what our response will be.

This passage contains a hymn, which the Philippian believers sang to express their understanding of who Jesus was and what he did. These words would have been common to the Philippian church. It's an ancient hymn born out of an immediate and particular realization of Jesus's majesty and humility.

We sing hymns today, too, to remind ourselves of what is true. Music has a way of cutting to the soul, of speaking to us in ways that prose sometimes cannot.

What did Paul sing? What was Jesus's journey? Where is our joy?

The Sadness of Where We Are

In Chapter 1, Paul discussed how the church is to remain in love and stand strong in the Gospel. But how? Through the encouragement in Christ, the comfort from love, the participation in the Spirit, and by affection and sympathy. Paul wants those attributes in the life of the church, in the community of saints. It's a vision of having the same mind, the same joy—being one together. Paul wants to see all the parts of the body functioning together in unison. This would bring him joy. In fact, it would complete his joy. Paul is talking about the unique power of unity.

There is something powerful and inspiring when a football team is firing on all cylinders. There is something thrilling when everyone hits his or her lines in a school play or notes in a band performance. There is something so satisfying when a team project comes together.

But there is a problem, and it's a big one. It's the buzzkill of this passage. Sure, we want to see perfect unity, hope, joy, and community. However, we don't often see it. It's elusive. Why is this so hard to hold onto?

Paul speaks to this in his admonition in Philippians 2:3 when he says, *"Do nothing from selfish ambition or conceit."* We disrupt joyful unison with selfish ambition and vain conceit. We break up our communities. We hurt each other. We use each other emotionally and physically. We destroy reputations. We count ourselves first and best. We promote only ourselves and our friends. We look only to the interests of our neighborhoods with NIMBY (Not In My Back Yard) policies. Can we acknowledge this selfish ambition and conceit in our hearts?

Many of us are good at covering up these problems and acting nice. We have developed social skills to mask the deep-seated selfishness of our lives, which is not an entirely bad thing. It's good that we aren't as selfish as we could be all the time. Most of us aren't. But the danger is that we might start to believe our own press and forget to be honest with ourselves about the fact that we believe our lives actually do revolve around our needs, our wants, and our desires. It's not always the worst-case scenario. We often hurt people subtly. It's not always obvious or blatant or even noticeable. But it's there.

If you are older than twenty, you likely have few restrictive boundaries in your life. You have disposable income. You have material possessions. You have free time. You have little supervision. You have privileges that go far beyond what most people in the world have. What do you do with all of those resources at your disposal? And when you help others, do you do so in order to put it on your resume or knock off your service hours?

All of us achievers work hard to stand out, to measure up, and to get to the top. If we can't do it with our GPAs, then it will have to be with our work ethic, or our networking, or our social savvy. We have to figure out some way to pat ourselves on the backs, especially when no one else is giving us the credit we think we deserve. Pride is a beast.

Overachieving is exhausting, so some of us give up, figuring negative attention is better than no attention at all. We can be proud of our rebellion. We can be proud that we're sticking it to the man or not following the rules. We can be proud that we're cynical and disbelieving and we've resisted being duped by the conformist majority. We're proud that we're out of shape, bad to the bone, and rocking the suburbs. We're attempting to be exceptional at not being exceptional.

The truth is we're all proud. Strife and rivalry are what we get as we interact with the world and other people. It's our college and pro teams that hate each other. It's the jocks versus the nerds. It's the Montagues versus the Capulets. It's the haves versus the have-nots. It's white versus black. It's my political party versus yours. It's my denomination versus yours.

Let me mention one other way we hurt people. We ignore them. We just let them go. We don't pursue them. The word for this indifference is "whatever." The opposite of love isn't hate. It's indifference. It's ignoring. It's —whatever.

Indifference is passing people without looking at them. It's consuming others. It's the dominant culture taking everything for granted. It's making decisions based on the bottom line rather than the common good. It's walling ourselves off from others and considering it an accomplishment. This indifference is one thing many people hate about the church.

Do you care about others? Do you care about people not like you—who look, think, talk, and act differently than you?

Conceit and vainglory lie behind all these actions. Stop for a minute and consider that the problem with your life might not be the president or the governor or the mayor. It may not be the taxation rate. It may not be the coach or the team. It may not be your teacher. It may not be your boss. It may not be your mom or your dad or your spouse or your grandkids. It may not be your church or your pastor. It may not be your neighbor.

The problem might just be *you* (and me).

We are each the common denominators of the problems around us. When we move roommates and majors and spouses and houses and cities and jobs—we still have problems. They follow us around, because it's not just everyone else that's the problem; it's *us*.

When we finally recognize we are the problem, we

may feel guilty and ashamed. The Avett Brothers express this in their song "Shame," which goes:

Shame
Boatloads of shame
Day after day
More of the same
Blame
Please lift it off
Please take it off
Please make it stop

When we see it and realize it, we feel the guilt, shame, and blame of our actions. We haven't lived in community like we should, like God calls us to in Philippians. We haven't loved like we should. We haven't participated in the Spirit. We don't have sympathy for others. In fact we have schadenfreuden, which is the German word for when someone gets joy from another's suffering. I love it when the Cubs and Jayhawks lose (how did the Cubs win the World Series?!). If I can't do well, then I'm just fine with others not doing well. I have a list: Cubs, Jayhawks, Longhorns, Wolverines, Fighting Irish, any team in the SEC, and more. I love to root against some teams!

As we become more honest with ourselves, we realize we're not good people. We might not be breaking all the social rules, but we are hurting others. So there is shame. There is blame. And we cry out—please take it off. Please make it stop.

Is this where you are? Have you made that cry? Have you seen and felt the weight of your lies, your shame, and your blame? Where do you go for help?

The Hope of Where We're Headed

I want you to sit with those questions for a minute. We will talk about how to cast off your shame and guilt, but first I want to look to the end of this passage in Philippians.

Read what Paul says about where we are going at the end of all things as we know it, which is also the beginning of the way things will always be. Paul says, *"Therefore God has highly exalted him and bestowed on him the name that is above every name, so that at the name of Jesus every knee should bow, in heaven and on earth and under the earth, and every tongue confess that Jesus Christ is Lord, to the glory of God the Father"* (Phil. 2:9–11). This passage points toward what is to come. There is a future ahead of us that is going to be magnificent, beyond what we can imagine.

Think of the best places you've been. I've been privileged to travel around the world and see incredible sites. Some of them have been buildings and cities that people have made. Others have been natural settings like mountains, oceans, forests, and lakes. I recently took a trip to Salt Lake City. I'd never been to Utah before, and it was stunning, filled with incredible natural beauty. I loved my time there.

Think of something you are looking forward to. Maybe it is Christmas break, or spring break, or summer break, or vacation, or marriage, or your first child, or your first grandchild, or starting your business, or retirement. The Bible tells us we're headed to a day that will be more glorious than any of those days. It will be way better than Utah.

On this day, everything will be set right and all will be made new. We will all be sitting at the feet of Jesus, the servant king of love. We will bow to him in honor and adoration.

It will be true glory. All present glories point to this true, future glory. This world is not as it should be, but when we get a glimpse of something glorious and great, we get a taste of what is to come. Those glimpses may be the goose bumps you get at your child's musical, or when you hear everyone cheering before kickoff, or when a baby is born, or when we witness a magnificent sunset.

Does your worldview include such hopefulness? Does it include the possibility of perfect justice and peace? Do you have a resolution to the storyline of the world? In your view of things, where does the story ultimately end? What are little things and the big things in life that bring you joy?

One of my favorite movies is *Where the Wild Things Are*, based on the 338-word children's book (that's not very many words for a book!). The movie explores why Max goes away to the island of the wild things. His mom is dating someone. He gets picked on by other kids. He's taught at school that the universe will be consumed when the sun burns out and collapses on itself. All will die. All will be hot and burning and dark and cold and—gone. Max feels overwhelmed and hopeless. He wonders what the point is of living each day. He escapes to the island of the wild things to process what is going on in his head and heart. He fights to believe that there is a place where hope and joy matter and are true. We all want this. We were made to want this.

I've learned about joy and hope from the black church. As a white male in our society, I have experienced a great deal of privilege and relatively little suffering. When I sat with one thousand black saints at the Martin Luther King Jr. service last January, I wept. I felt both incredible sadness and hope.

I didn't merely watch people sing "We Shall Overcome." I sang it with them. I questioned initially whether I had the right to be singing this song of hope born out of injustice. Yet this hope and gladness also made sense to me as I sang. It helped form me. I was sad about our country's shameful past and present struggles with racial inequality *and* hopeful that God would continue to make all things new. I wanted to be part of that happening! I appreciated the struggle and joy in a different way.

Paul calls us to a joyful hope in the midst of struggle as we eagerly anticipate the ultimate joyful climax of eternity in heaven. He says there will be a time and a place of joy. Our vast historic journey will end not in Utah, not at the altar, not in the labor and delivery room, and not at a retirement party. It will end in a forever future with the gracious loving Creator Redeemer King for all those who are his. That is what Paul is pointing to in Philippians 2.

Someday all the slices of heaven that we experience in this life will come together in the new heavens and new earth. It will be amazing, it will be glorious, and it will most certainly be joyful!

How We Get There

We have against the backdrop of a passage about pride and self-centeredness one of the great passages of the Bible about who Jesus is and what he has done. It's how we get from the sadness of where we are to the hope of where we're going. We get there through Jesus.

First, Paul reminds us in Philippians 2 that Jesus is God. He teaches us that Jesus was preeminent. He existed long before he was born as a baby in a manger. In fact, he existed before time. The Apostle John writes, *"In the beginning was the Word, and the Word was with God, and the Word was God"* (John. 1:1). Jesus was not created. He is the second person in the Trinity, existing from all time. This is a remarkable (and mysterious) assertion, which no other religion makes.

Paul echoes other biblical authors here to say Jesus is equal with God. When Philippians 2:6 says Jesus *"did not count equality with God a thing to be grasped,"* it means Jesus didn't have to scramble and fight for his place or position. He had it. He was it. It's not like there is CEO God and Junior Partner Jesus. They are equal. They, along with the Holy Spirit, have different roles in the Trinity, but they accept those roles willingly in the economy of the Godhead, not out of a difference in stature.

But—and this is also big—Jesus became a man. He was God, but he made himself nothing, *"taking the form of a servant, being born in the likeness of men"* (Phil. 2:7). Now it might sound like Jesus just looked like a man, like the man part was an outer shell for him. But this text isn't saying that. It means that he was all God *and* all man.

One ancient creed people have used for centuries (dating back to 325 AD) is the Nicene Creed. This creed is very particular about getting Jesus correct. It says:

> I believe in one God, the Father Almighty, Maker of heaven and earth, and of all things visible and invisible.
>
> And in one Lord Jesus Christ, the only-begotten Son of God, begotten of the Father before all worlds; God of God, Light of Light, very God of very God; begotten, not made, being of one substance with the Father, by whom all things were made; who for us men and for our salvation came down from heaven and was incarnate by the Holy Spirit of the virgin Mary and was made man; and was crucified also for us under Pontius Pilate. He suffered and was buried. And the third day He rose again according to the Scriptures and ascended into heaven and sits at the right hand of the Father.
>
> And He will come again with glory to judge both the

living and the dead, whose kingdom will have no end. And I believe in the Holy Spirit, the Lord and giver of life, who proceeds from the Father and the Son, who with the Father and the Son together is worshiped and glorified, who spoke by the prophets. And I believe in one holy catholic and apostolic Church, I acknowledge one Baptism for the remission of sins, and I look for the resurrection of the dead and the life of the world to come. Amen.

The Apostles' Creed is another important ancient creed. It says of Jesus, "He was born of the virgin Mary." God came down. God came to earth. God was implanted into the womb of a woman. God developed in a first trimester and a second trimester and came to full term and was born. He nursed. He grew up. He had to learn to speak and to read. He worked. He got tired. He was happy and sad. God loved the world so much that he sent his son into the world so he could redeem the world.

So on the one hand, we have the Christmas story, which is also called the Incarnation. A name for Jesus, Immanuel, means "God with us." God cared enough about us and our world that he sent his son to be born into poverty and lowliness, to live a life just like we lived, to obey God in every way, and to suffer and die the worst death imaginable, and to rise again from the dead —for us!

God could have come down as a Roman emperor, or an Egyptian pharaoh, or an American president. I only know those would not have been better because they didn't happen. I trust that God's plan was the best one. Jesus was born in Bethlehem to a young woman named Mary. He grew up in obscurity until he started his public ministry at the age of thirty.

So this passage doesn't just suggest Christmas, but it

also points to Good Friday and Easter, to the cross, to the crucifixion, and then to the resurrection. The Apostles' Creed says in part: Jesus was born of the virgin Mary and suffered under Pontius Pilate. He was crucified, died, and was buried. He descended into hell. He was raised again on the third day. He ascended into heaven.

Paul tells us Jesus came as a servant and *"humbled himself by becoming obedient to the point of death, even death on a cross"* (Phil. 2:8).

We all have formed some perception of Jesus in our minds. What is your conception of Jesus? Is he open-minded or closed-minded? Is he a hippie or a yuppy, or white or black, or all love or all hate? Does Jesus hate religion? Is he sponsoring family values or is he a revolutionary? Can we define him as we wish? Can we separate him from our culture?

We need to let our perceptions be formed by Scripture and we aware of our cultural biases. We can't avoid having cultural perceptions, but we can be aware of them in order to not be blind to them.

Paul is telling us in this passage about Jesus Christ the Son of the living God. He is the glory of God. He wasn't just some guy walking around talking about things. He wasn't just a teacher who was misunderstood. He wasn't just a revolutionary who happened to gain traction. He was God himself, come in the flesh, to live and die for you and for me.

There are so many things we could say about this passage, but let me just say one more. Do you see what God did for us, for you? He came down. He moved into our neighborhood. He dwelled among us. God did.

He moved in himself. This isn't selfish ambition or vain conceit. This isn't active hate. Nor is it a passive, ignoring hate. This isn't rivalry. This is love.

Think of your least favorite job or chore. Think of the

thing you most hate to do. I can tell you one of mine. I absolutely despise plunging the toilet. I don't think I need to go into an explanation of why that is. I cannot handle it, and sometimes I have to do it.

Do you think Bill Gates plunges his own toilet? I would guess not. Do you think he would plunge someone else's toilet? I doubt it. What if I lived in the apartment complex Bill Gates owned, and I called up and needed help, and he showed up with a plunger in his hand, ready to get smelly and dirty?

That doesn't even come close to the enormous, incredible, awe-inspiring fact that Jesus, God himself, came to live and dwell among us, to get dirty, to move into our neighborhood, to be with us, to get smelly and dirty for us, in order to save us.

You need to think about that truth and its ramifications. If you understand that, you can't just "like" Jesus. People in the Bible either loved Jesus or hated him. He didn't produce "like" in people. They wanted to either crown him or crucify him. There was very little in between.

You could use that idea as a diagnosis of sorts. If you like Jesus, then maybe you are liking and following a Jesus other than the one described in the Scriptures. You could be following the Republican Jesus or the Democrat Jesus or the Hipster Jesus or the Free Love Jesus. But I would bet it's not the Real Jesus. The real Jesus is much more troubling, soul-disturbing, and foundation-shifting than we often think. Following the real Jesus is going to involve sacrificial love, radical forgiveness, suffering, stretching boundaries.

Do you know this real Jesus, the one Paul's talking about in Philippians 2? Jesus used his power to serve. He has all at his disposal, all the riches of heaven and earth.

He owns and created it all. Yet he gave it up to become a servant, to die a death on a cross.

This is who we go to for our guilt and shame problems. To Jesus. Nothing else will ever take care of the core of the problem. Jesus will. Jesus forgives us. He heals us. He loves us. He restores us. We find our rest in him. He is where we go for new life and a directional aspect for our virtues and motivations. He is where we go in order to find out how to live *his* way. It's a whole new life, a whole new direction, a whole new motivation.

Look to Jesus. Look to his life. Look to his teachings. Look to his death. Do you understand this love? Are you compelled by it? Does it move you? Look to the resurrection. Look to his glorification when he returns and we enter into his fullness.

The Avett Brothers sing in "I and Love and You," "Three words that became hard to say: I and love and you." Those words are hard to say because you know if you say them, you have to do something about it. You have to give your life to that person, all of it. That's the meaning of love. It's sacrificing and dying to yourself for someone else.

Why It Matters Now

Philippians 2:1–11 remains relevant today. First, embracing Christ and following his example of humility is our only hope to correct our pride, the rivalry and conceit that plague us. We could be tempted to hunker down and work hard to "do better." We might see our faults and try to correct them because we feel bad about who we really are. So we might have lunch with someone out of our peer group or start to wear skinny jeans or North Face fleeces or try new culturally relevant things.

But it won't work. It won't last. True transformation doesn't come from just our own efforts.

We are called to love people, all sorts of people. Everyone is our neighbor. The ability to love comes from Christ. We look to him and his love for us, which then transforms us. The Gospel changes us, as it changes everything. It breaks down the walls of rivalry and division and conceit in our hearts, so we can then love others. Gospel change is powerful enough to overcome as seemingly insurmountable an obstacle as our country's past and present racial tensions to bring about genuine reconciliation.

When the Gospel changes us, we see the world differently, and we aren't the center of the universe anymore. Jesus is! His agenda is our agenda. This means we can risk things. We can let people into our spaces, our homes, our churches. We don't have to exclusively be around people who look like us or think like us. We can admit we don't have everything figured out. We can acknowledge that life involves pain and suffering and confusion and sorrow, but also joy and hope and confirmation and love.

The fact that Jesus came into the world is profound; the life he lived on earth was different from what we're used to. He was friends with sinners. He hung out with Pharisees, but also with prostitutes, lepers, and others with questionable reputations. People accused him of blaspheming God. He did miracles on the Sabbath and people thought that was not OK.

Because of Jesus' love, we can love others, in our families, neighborhoods, cities, world. You could join a group where you are a minority. You could move into a community to encourage and serve the people there. You could volunteer to tutor kids, make soup for someone who is sick, ask someone out to lunch, join a team outside of your normal friend group, attend a concert with someone you work with, walk around your block to meet people, give someone a ride to the doctor, advocate for those who are outside of the system, do someone's hair for prom, or sit next to someone alone in church.

The Avett Brothers' "Salvation Song" is one of my favorites:

We came for salvation
We came for family
We came for all that's good and that's how we'll walk away
We came to break the bad
We came to cheer the sad
We came to leave behind the world a better way

We used to put those lyrics at the bottom of the bulletin for each church service at City Pres. We came for salvation! Salvation is why we meet to worship every week, isn't it? It's why we sing these songs and open the Scriptures together. It's why we meet in small groups throughout the week. It's why we go and do things. It's why we get married and have kids. It's why we ask for forgiveness in repentance. It's why we care about our city. It's why we open our church to other events that don't seem like they pertain to the mission and vision of what we normally call church. Because of Philippians 2.

Everyone will eventually bow the knee to Jesus. Everyone. Will you do so willingly or begrudgingly?

Paul bowed his knee in dramatic fashion. You can read about his conversion in Acts 9. Paul hated Christianity. He had studied the Scriptures backward and forward, so he was very knowledgeable and articulate in his opposition. He was even killing Christians before Jesus broke through to him on the road to Damascus. Then Paul was radically changed.

Jesus is calling all of us to love and follow him. Some

of us need to make dramatic changes in our lives. We need to bow the knee to Jesus altogether or in some specific area of our lives. Something has to change. The time is now. Jesus is Lord, and we need to actually follow him.

Even though my journey to Eagle Lake Camp to propose to Julie was long and the outcome unsure, I looked forward to it, which was far easier than his. Like him, I also was asking a bride to marry me—though I didn't have to die like he did. I suppose in a sense I was laying down my life for hers, but it's such a pale comparison.

Our marriage has had its ups and downs, as Julie would agree. She might have turned me down if she had really known what she was getting into. I got the far better end of the deal. Marriages are filled with disappointments and grief and yet also with love and joy.

Jesus didn't dread his journey, even though he knew what would be involved. He gave up so much to come and marry his bride, his church. But he came to seek and to save the lost. His journey of love and joy was as a Savior, who came to give his life for his people, so that they could have true life.

EVERYDAY, NORMAL, MUNDANE JOY

PHILIPPIANS 2:12-30

Even if I am to be poured out as a drink offering upon the
sacrificial offering of your faith, I am glad and rejoice with you
all. Likewise you also should be glad and
rejoice with me.
—Philippians. 2:17–18

We're talking about the birth and life of joy through the book of Philippians. Paul wrote this letter to the church at Philippi around 62 AD under circumstances we would consider the antithesis of joyful: he was imprisoned in Rome, under house arrest, chained to a palace guard. He wrote to a church he loved, to his friends. They cared for him, too, and sent him aid, help, and comfort.

Philippi was an outpost military town where Romans sent their ex-military men and their families after the men retired so Rome could have a presence in the hinterland. Imagine a place like Carson City, Nevada, with some soldiers sent there to keep the peace.

In the last part of Chapter 2, we see Paul's travelogue. Right after his incredible message about Jesus's divinity and humanity in the first part of the chapter, we get

Paul's instructions to be obedient and then detailed infor-mation about who went where when and what they did. We abruptly move from the theological to the practical. And then we go even beyond practical living and into the details of his travel schedule.

How important is this? Should we care about this? I (Doug) think yes! This passage shows how Paul's theology works itself out in everyday life. We can talk about the super highs and super lows of our spiritual journeys, but most of our time is spent traveling the vast space between those two extremes.

Not long ago, I downloaded an app that tracks my sleep. When I looked at it recently, it said I had 284 nights of data recorded. My average night of sleep is seven hours and thirty-three minutes. When I add up those minutes, I spent thirteen recorded weeks asleep! Sleep adds up. The average person will rack up twenty-six *years* of sleep over a lifetime.

You can start to wonder how many days and hours you spend doing incredibly ordinary things, such as sleeping, working, or watching TV, among other things. The average British person (the article I found focused on the Brits)[1] spends six months of his or her life standing in line, four years on the phone at work, and twenty weeks on hold. If you average four hours a day, all of that televi-sion watching adds up to eleven years in front of the TV. If you complain eight minutes every day, you'll accumu-late five months of bellyaching in your life. Ordinary things add up.

Do we really want to give an official account of our ordinary, mundane lives? They don't make good press, do they? As a campus minister and church planter, I've given many reports about ministry in my day. I usually only have a few minutes, and everyone wants to hear a dramatic, amazing story. I'm thankful to have some amazing, dramatic stories, but I just as honestly could say, "We are going about the normal, everyday, routine, mundane things. That takes up 99 percent of my ministry. The exciting parts amount to one percent. The means of grace are working. We pray. We preach. We sing. We meet together. We talk. We listen. We take the Lord's Supper. We believe this is what it takes. Thank you very much for your time." I'd sit down, and I don't know if I would be asked to share again if I said that, but it would be true.

In the end of Philippians 2, Paul gives us an even more boring report. He moves from the dramatic heights of Jesus's journey of love to the mechanics of his own travel. In just a few paragraphs, we go from the most incredible journey ever known (the incarnational ministry of Jesus) to the mundane, everyday, obedient Christian life. What can we learn from this?

Obedience

Paul is calling us to live a life that flows out of the life of Christ. Paul has been talking about a time in the future when every knee will bow and every tongue will confess that Jesus Christ is Lord (Phil. 2:1–11). This is an eternal future where nothing will ever go wrong again. There will be no death, no suffering, no tears, and no sadness. In fact, all wrongs will be set right. So it will be a place of justice and rightness. And it will be a place of love.

We're headed to that place, which is all about Jesus and his work. But it's not only about Jesus. All those who love Jesus will be there with him. So this future day and place is about you and me and this world and all of us. It's about the earth and our cultures and societies and histories. Because of that future day, all of this life matters. We're connected to that future day. This day and every day is a part of that redemptive, eternal future.

Paul wants us to connect to that redemptive story and its trajectory. He doesn't want us to just get our "Get into heaven free" card, which is also the "Get out of hell free" card. He's telling us that the good news that Christ saves sinners has an impact in the future and *now*. He wants us to be a people of faith in the sacrificial life and death of Jesus. He keeps saying that if this Gospel message is true, then we will live differently now. It will impact our lives now.

Paul wants us to obey Christ as we follow him. What we love and seek impacts our daily lives in a tangible way. As we imitate those who follow Christ, Paul tells us in Philippians 2:12–18 to also be glad and rejoice with him:

Therefore, my beloved, as you have always obeyed, so now, not only as in my presence but much more in my absence, work out your own salvation with fear and trembling, for it is God who works in you, both to will and to work for his good pleasure. Do all things without grumbling or disputing, that you may be blameless and innocent, children of God without blemish in the midst of a crooked and twisted generation, among whom you shine as lights in the world, holding fast to the word of life, so that in the day of Christ I may be proud that I did not run in vain or labor in vain. Even if I am to be poured out as a drink offering upon the sacrificial offering of your faith, I am glad and rejoice with you all. Likewise you also should be glad and rejoice with me.

Living an obedient Christian life likely means we start doing some things, we keep doing some things, and we stop doing other things. I find it more helpful to focus on what we're supposed to do rather than on what we're not supposed to do. These are habits and practices that form our hearts, our desires, and our affections. So what is

Paul saying our obedient life in Gospel hope and love ought to consist of?

Obedience Instead of Anarchy

Therefore, my beloved, as you have always obeyed, so now, not only as in my presence but much more in my absence.
—Philippians 2:12

We show our love by our obedience. Obedience doesn't earn us love. That's an important distinction. We don't earn God's favor through our good works. We can't merit God's love by doing right things. There is no righteousness available to us except for Christ's. If you think you can ever, ever do enough enough to earn God's favor, you are wrong!

The Bible tells us over and over that we are rebels. We hate God. We may act all nice, but in our hearts and minds we resist his authority over our lives. We want to do what we want to do.

But God can change us. He gives us forgiveness and redeems us. He puts our evil thoughts, words, and deeds onto Jesus, and he puts Jesus's righteous thoughts, words, and deeds onto us. Then, when God looks at us he sees Jesus's life of perfect obedience instead of our lives of disobedience. He sees Jesus's death and counts it for our deaths—if you are in Christ and he is in you.

It is impossible to stop there. If Jesus and the Holy Spirit are in you, that Gospel message changes everything in your life. If you love Christ, you cannot work at cross purposes with him, his love, and his rule. It may take time, and it isn't a tidy, linear, always-forward process, but if you love something, you will fit it into your life—no matter what, whatever it takes.

If I love my wife, Julie, then I make the effort to put her needs and wants before my own. If I love my kids, then I will spend time with them and sacrifice for them. If I love my church, then I will make time for it and help it whatever the cost. If I love running, then I buy the shoes, sign up for the race, and commit to the training program. If I love gaming, then I stay up all night playing. You get the idea. We conform our lives to what we love. We sacrifice our time for what we love. Even those who seem like they are slackers and can't get anything done actually are very committed to things when they have passion and love for them. As we walk with and follow Jesus, we grow to love the things he loves.

We have to commit to something even before we totally understand it and then follow those rules and learn those ways. If you obey the rules of your passion, you'll develop more passion, not less. You'll understand painting better if you study it and sit underneath those who know more about it than you do. As you run more miles, you begin to nurture a devotion to running you didn't know before. If you keep doing something out of an obedience to it, you'll grow in your understanding and appreciation of that subject, that thing, or that person. And you may fall in love with it. Obedience and love are two-way streets. We need both directions for it to flow the way it's supposed to.

Salvation Instead of Servitude

> *…Work out your own salvation with fear and trembling.*
> —Philippians 2:12

This phrase "work out your own salvation with fear and trembling" has given a lot of people trouble over the years. There is no way we can earn God's favor in order to merit our own salvation, but here it sounds like Paul is saying that very thing—*work out* your own salvation.

We know Paul doesn't mean our salvation comes through our works because he is fervently against a works-based salvation everywhere else in his writing. Ephesians 2:8–9 says: *"For by grace you have been saved through faith. And this is not your own doing; it is the gift of God, not a result of works, so that no one may boast."*

You cannot work *out* your salvation unless it is already worked *in*. We are not to work *for* our salvation. We're to work it *out*. The theological term for this is sanctification. The answer to question thirty-five of the Westminster Shorter Catechism teaches, "Sanctification is the work of God's free grace, whereby we are renewed in the whole man after the image of God, and are enabled more and more to die unto sin and live unto righteousness."

Once we have Christ in our lives, we need to continue to explore how the Gospel changes us. We need to continually consider how Christ can be glorified in every aspect of our lives. When we see things in our lives that don't conform to the Gospel, we repent and change them. We grow in our interest in the Bible, in singing hymns, in prayers, in community, in church and worship, in sermons, in reading good books and discussing them, in serving others. We turn away from or die to the things that hurt us, hurt God, and hurt others. We need to pursue the things of the Spirit. All this is part of working out our salvation. Yet ultimately our sanctification is still a work of God. We participate with him *in* it, while giving him the credit *for* it.

Let me also mention this "fear and trembling" part. Paul is tapping into his Old Testament knowledge, using words and phrases from God's history with his people. Having fear and trembling doesn't mean cowering in a corner and never coming to God. But I don't think cowering is our modern problem; it's casualness. We often think we can walk into God and his presence any way we choose. After all, he loves us, right? He doesn't care what we wear, what we do, or what we say.

On the one hand, yes. We can come to God any way we want, for we are his children. On the other hand, we are to respect God. He is almighty. He is omnipotent. He is omniscient. He is holy. He is everything good! We should respect that in the way we come to him and talk to him. Not in a fake way, but in a way that acknowledges him as king of the universe. We should then also think seriously about how our salvation is being worked out. A little more fear and trembling probably wouldn't hurt any of us as we move forward in obedience.

Work for God's Good Pleasure Instead of Our Credit or Shame

. . . for it is God who works in you, both to will and to work for his good pleasure. —Philippians. 2:13

We work out our salvation, but ultimately it is God's work in us that enables us to do so. We're not left on our own in some self-improvement program. We have his will, and we have his work, which ensures progress can happen.

Some of you tend toward activism. Your motto is, "Let's go for it!" You want me to give you a list of obedient behaviors so you can write them down and start working on them this minute. Your pen is at the ready for those bullet points and nothing else really registers for you. You want to do lists and activities and checked boxes.

Others of you are quietists. You hate lists! You don't trust action and instead adopt the motto of "Let go and let God." You want to let God work it out over time. You already feel overwhelmed and ready to give up.

Paul doesn't agree with either camp. He wants us to work out our salvation, yes. But he also knows and believes the foundation of this is something outside of us. We can't just change by relying on our own efforts. God changes us. We have to participate in the change, but he changes us.

At the end of the day, it is God's work, not ours. We can't take the credit. We can't even take the credit for our own salvation. He did it. He does it. He will do it. For his glory, not ours.

Who brought you to salvation? God. Who believed in Christ and had faith in him? You. Who is the one who is supposed to pray? You. Does prayer work just because you do it? No, prayer works because of God. Why do we have the church? God! But the church needs to be faithful and brave, committed to truth and love. Why do we have worship? God.

The ultimate source of everything is God. He is the one working and willing for his good pleasure because he loves us. Do we know that? Do we believe that?

We tend to either take all the credit for ourselves and think we are the heroes of the story, or we don't believe there can be change at all, that God isn't powerful enough to do anything about our situation. We feel ashamed we're not far enough along and guilty that we're still bad people.

The third way—Paul's way— is to believe that God loves us, *and* he changes people. We can be new creations, which means the Holy Spirit is in us and his power is living and active in our lives. His power works for his good pleasure, not for ours, although we can take pleasure in it because he is pleased.

———————

Kindness and Trust Instead of Grumbling and Disputing

> *Do all things without grumbling*
> *or disputing...* —Philippians 2:14

Paul loves the Philippians, and because he loves them he tells them in this verse about something that is wrong with their lives. As they're working out their salvation with fear and trembling, as God works that out for them for his good pleasure, they have to be careful about the poison in their midst. It's not just stale water. It's not just bitter beer. It's not just flat soda. It's poison that kills. The poison is grumbling and disputing.

Paul is again referencing the Old Testament. The Israelites were particularly known for their grumbling in their interactions with God. If you read from Exodus on, you'll see what huge complainers they were. They had just been released from a lifetime of brutal captivity as Egyptian slaves. They were free! But they still complained like crazy. They didn't think they had enough food or water, so they asked Moses, "Did you bring us out here to die?"

On the one hand, it was a fair question. They were really struggling and didn't know what to do. On the other hand, God had just parted the Red Sea and defeated the Egyptians before their very eyes. Was he really not strong enough to feed them and take care of them? Didn't they forget his care that quickly?

But we are the same way. Nothing is ever good

enough. We complain about the people around us, whether it's our friends, spouses, kids, bosses, class-mates, teachers, or local sports team. Anything is fair game to complain about at the drop of a hat.

Sports channels, especially talk radio formats, are more interesting when there is a controversy to discuss, so the announcers often stir up dissatisfaction. People are mad about the coaching, the players, every little thing. Contentment is not a characteristic of sports radio; nor is it a characteristic of our hearts. We like to give our opin-ions, and we love to complain and argue and grumble.

I think all of us are really, ultimately, deep down mad at God about something. That's why we complain and grumble so much. We think it's God's fault we are unhappy or struggling. He could have given us different friends, circumstances, parents, bodies, personalities. We mistakenly think that if we had different circumstances, we wouldn't grumble or complain.

Grumbling not only kills Gospel joy in our own hearts, but it kills community, too. It's not wrong to discuss or ask questions, especially with an open mind and attitude willing to listen, learn, and change. But often we don't assume the best or take a grace-filled perspec-tive. We just want to grumble and complain.

We need to learn to be content and thankful. We also need to learn how to have conversations and even disputes where our voices are heard and then dealt with, even if we don't think the results are the right ones. We need to be able to handle our disagreements with respect, dignity, and honor. We need to listen to others whose opinions differ from ours and consider what it's like not to feel understood, listened to, taken seriously, or befriended. We need to forgive when we hurt each other. We need to take everything to Jesus and ask him for wisdom and guidance, as well as courage and grace.

Blameless Instead of Corrupted

> *. . . that you may be blameless and innocent, children of God*
> *without blemish.* —Philippians 2:15

Paul calls us to trade in our grumbling hearts and lives for ones that are blameless and innocent. He wants us to find ourselves in Christ. This discrepancy between where we are and where we should be is what drives us to Christ. We cannot be blameless and without sin by ourselves. However, we can be considered blameless and innocent children of God if Christ is in us and we are in him.

How can we be "blameless and innocent, children of God without blemish"? We can seek to treat others with respect, honor, and love. We can ask for forgiveness when we mess up. We can demonstrate integrity through our actions and words. We can stop sinning just because we think it's OK and God will forgive us. We can stop the gossip. We can evaluate what we do with our time, money, and bodies. Then we can go deeper. We can ask God to reveal to us the sins we are currently blind to. Remember, he has the will and the power to change us for good.

Children of God Instead of Orphans

> *...children of God...* —Philippians 2:15

We are to live out the reality of our lives as children of God. If we are a Christian, then we have been adopted by

God into the family of God. He is our father. This is our new identity.

Many of us think we have this status as children of God because we are so good and worthy. We have this idea that God picked us because we are so amazing, and he is happy and privileged to have us on his team. We're like the first pick in the draft.

That's the wrong picture. Amazing grace should drive us to our knees with wonder that God would pick us. We were children of Adam—wicked, corrupt, sinful, rebellious, spiteful, hateful, ungrateful wretches. But God still loved us. He still came to us and worked in us to will and to work for his good pleasure. We love him because he first loved us. The Son of Man came to seek and to save that which was lost. Christ came for sinners!

When we are saved by grace we get a new identity. We are adopted into the family of God and given a new name: Christian. God loves us so much. He doesn't just tolerate us. He's not rolling his eyes at us. He is crazy about us!

This is a relational truth, which is important to remember. We need to live out of our identity as loved children of God. Too often we instead live as though we are orphans. We live like we've been abandoned. We live like we're destitute and dropped off.

But we have riches. We have wealth beyond measure. We have power because we have a powerful Father. We have strength. We have honor. We have dignity. We have everything in him. Remember that. You are a son; you are a daughter of the king! So we're called to live our lives as loved, loving, grateful, thankful, obedient children.

Lights Instead of Darkness

...without blemish in the midst of a crooked and twisted
generation, among whom you shine as lights in the world,
holding fast to the word of life, so that in the day of Christ I
may be proud that I did not run in vain or labor in vain.
—Philippians 2:15–16

Paul switches metaphors here, moving to another Old Testament reference, this time in Genesis. God talked to Abraham and told him how he planned to change the world through Abraham's old, worn-out body. God would use Abraham to people the earth with his lineage. Abraham's descendants would be like stars in the sky, like sand on the seashore. God promised Abraham he would accomplish these things through a son he would miraculously give him in his old age. When God promised these things to Abraham, he told him to look up to the stars, the lights in the sky in the midst of the darkness.

We live in the midst of a crooked and depraved generation. That has *always* been true. Bad people have done bad things throughout history, since Adam and Eve. Don't believe it when your parents or grandparents tell you things were better back in the day. Some things were better. Some things were worse. But really they were just different. The crookedness and depravity is still just as strong as it ever was, but it does manifest itself in different ways in different ages. You would be wise to figure out what those ways are today and how they control and manipulate you in ways you may not even realize.

As Christians, we are supposed to be lights in the darkness of the world. God calls us to hold up hope, justice, goodness, faithfulness, chastity, grace, forgiveness, and service—for his glory, not ours.

Another church in our city has the motto: "Love God.

Love People. Push Back Darkness." As lights, we want to push back the darkness all around us, in our own hearts and in the lives of others. We don't want to judge others and call them to morality. Instead, we want to be lights in the darkness, pointing to God. Pushing back the darkness of people's lives means being there. We have to be present in the places where darkness exists. That shouldn't be too hard, since it's all around us. What are you offering to people around you? How are you helping to push back the darkness?

As you go, hold fast to the Word of Life, so your light will not be extinguished. Holding fast to the Word of Life is an offensive posture of evangelism, as we go into the darkness. Jesus said, *"I am the way, and the truth, and the life. No one comes to the Father except through me"* (John 14:6).

We obey God because we love God and know we are loved by God. Jesus said, we're to love God with all our heart, soul, mind, and strength and love our neighbor as ourselves (Mark 12:30–31). What do you think obedience means? Are you trying to live an obedient life?

We must follow Jesus, who said, *"If anyone would come after me, let him deny himself and take up his cross and follow me"* (Mark 8:34). What does it look like to follow Jesus like that? How is following Jesus changing you?

Jesus is the light of the world (John 8:12). He is the Son of God. He is the sacrifice for our sins. He obeyed the Father blamelessly. Salvation is found in no other. If you accept the finished work of Christ on your behalf, you can unleash the power of joy over the darkness. He is the one who lived the blameless life for you!

Imitation

Paul has been talking about the mind of Christ and how Jesus did not consider equality with God something to be grasped but took the very nature of a servant, even to death on the cross. Paul says we are to have that same mind with each other as we love and serve together in obedience to God. So the end of Chapter 2 flows out of the ministry, life, and example of Jesus.

Paul wants us to understand that Jesus Christ came to this world as God made flesh to live among us as a man, to obey the law perfectly, to die as the payment for our sins, and to rise again in new life, conquering death forever. If we understand and commit to that good news, it will result in a new life of discipleship and obedience for each of us. Paul goes on to tell us how that new life will look.

Paul says we should follow Jesus and look to him. He also says we should follow others who are following Christ. We should look to them and imitate them. Paul gives three examples of people to imitate. If we can't quite get our minds around obeying the Savior of the World, we can get a little closer to home by thinking about imitating the lives of three men. These were men the Philippians would have known.

The first person they can imitate is him. Paul says, *"Even if I am to be poured out as a drink offering upon the sacrificial offering of your faith, I am glad and rejoice with you all"* (Phil. 2:17). Paul gives himself up for the sake of others. He pours himself out and is willing to do so even to the point of death.

Paul next holds up Timothy. He says, *"I hope in the Lord Jesus to send Timothy to you soon, so that I too may be cheered by news of you. For I have no one like him, who will be genuinely concerned for your welfare. For they all seek their own interests, not those of Jesus Christ. But you know Timo-thy's proven worth, how as a son with a father he has served with me in the Gospel. I hope therefore to send him just as soon as I see how it will go with me, and I trust in the Lord that shortly I myself will come also"* (Phil. 2:19–24).

Paul says he has no one like Timothy, who genuinely seeks after the Philippians' welfare. He cares about them. He loves them. He wants their best, not just his best. He wants them to seek and to serve Jesus Christ. So Timothy is concerned for them, but he also is concerned for Jesus.

Timothy is like a son to Paul. More can be learned about their relationship by reading 1 Timothy and 2 Timothy in the New Testament. Timothy was a partner, church planter, and very close to Paul's heart as they served together in ministering the good news.

Because of these connections, Paul wants to send Timothy to the Philippians so he can work and live among them. Timothy has a heart for them, a heart for Jesus, and a heart for Paul, and he is sent to work in their midst as soon as he can get away. Paul commends Timothy as someone for us all to look up to and follow in this type of sacrifice and devotion.

The third example Paul gives to imitate is Epaphrodi-tus. Philippians 2:25–30 says:

I have thought it necessary to send to you Epaphroditus my brother and fellow worker and fellow soldier, and your messenger and minister to my need, for he has been longing for you all and has been distressed because you heard that he was ill. Indeed he was ill, near to death. But God had mercy on him, and not only on him but on me also, lest I should have sorrow upon sorrow. I am the more eager to send him, therefore, that you may rejoice at seeing him again, and that I may be less anxious. So receive him in the Lord with all joy, and honor such men, for he nearly died for the work of Christ,

*risking his life to complete what was lacking in your service
to me.*

We don't know much about Epaphroditus, but he comes on the scene unexpectedly and then fades away just as suddenly. However, Paul calls him a brother and fellow worker. Epaphroditus and Paul work together, side by side, for the sake of the Gospel. They have a common task. Paul also calls him a fellow soldier. Paul knows they are in spiritual battle, getting attacked from the outside and the inside. Paul is in jail for his faith. He is suffering, but he is not alone. Epaphroditus is standing beside him, ready to take on the attackers in a position of strength instead of weakness. Epaphroditus is a part of Paul's band of brothers. At one point, Epaphroditus almost even died on the way to visit Paul, but he pressed on because he cared for Paul and was devoted to serving Christ. Paul plans to send him back to the Philippians. Epaphroditus is living his life for others, for their good and not his own.

Imitation is often called the sincerest form of flattery. Imitation can be good or bad. We need to be sure we are imitating the right people and qualities, those that are in line with what pleases God.

A few years ago, my sons Cal and Drew both took extensive hitting lessons for baseball. The coach would watch them hit over and over. They'd work through drills. They'd get instruction. They'd practice and practice. The basic idea was there is a certain way to hit effectively. Each person can have his own style to some extent, but if you want to hit well, there are particular things you have to be able to do. Coming up with the most creative way to hit doesn't help hitting. You have to learn to hit the right way. You can argue and complain, but eventually, if you want to hit effectively, you have to learn how to do it the correct way. You have to imitate those who know how to hit this way. If you work at it, you likely will discover the joy of hitting as you begin to do it well. This skill is acquired through discipline, imitation, and practice.

Who are you imitating? Whom do you look up to? Who is influencing you for good? Who are your role models?

We need healthy, godly people to imitate—not famous ones—good models to know about and pattern our lives after. We need to imitate those who love their families well, rest well, eat well, give well, and forgive well. We need to imitate those who faithfully—though not perfectly—seek to imitate Christ. Paul named imperfect people (himself, Timothy, and Epaphroditus) and encourages us to imitate them. In Hebrews 11, we get the heroes hall of faith, and we're told to imitate their faith even though they were broken people.

Imitate those who trust in God and love him even when they're sick and suffering. Imitate those who walk into hard conversations for reconciliation. Imitate those who invite other people not like them into their homes. Imitate those who use their privilege for other people's good and not their own. Imitate those who live within their means and are even willing to experience downward mobility in order to help others. Imitate those who stay married. Imitate those who pursue spiritual disciplines for the glory of God. Imitate those who risk, trust, are humble, have joy. Find someone to imitate!

This is the way imitation in life works. We look to people. We are influenced by people. Who influences you? Whom do you influence?

Sacrifice

We could end right there, and some of us would feel pretty good. Obedience—check. Fellow workers—check. Imitate Paul—check. But knowing about these principles and doing them are not the same thing. When I give my son Cal an article about the football player from Stanford who starts on offense as a fullback and defense as a linebacker, he can be inspired, but then he still has to go out and play football himself.

Most of us are willing to sacrifice for ourselves. We will look out for number one, as we've been taught to do much our lives. We rarely make sacrifices for others, and when we do, sometimes it is only so we can feel good about ourselves in the end. We hate to suffer and often will go to great lengths to avoid pain.

We've often imitated the wrong people. We've chosen the wrong models, and instead of following Christ, we've become more hateful, more greedy, more addicted, more complacent, and more discontent. Yet Paul has given us three examples (Paul, Timothy, and Epaphroditus) who are giving up their lives for something bigger than themselves, for people, for God's church. Paul pours his life out like a drink offering, and he calls us to do the same.

In Philippians 2:17, Paul makes another Old Testament reference when he says, *"Even if I am to be poured out as a drink offering upon the sacrificial offering of your faith."* This refers to Numbers 28:7b, which says, *"In the Holy Place you shall pour out a drink offering of strong drink to the Lord."* A drink offering was something poured out for the sins of others. Paul is saying his life is poured out for the sake of others. He is covering their sins. He is giving up his rights and his life so they can live. This means Paul isn't only concerned with his pleasure. His joy is for them. His life is for them.

Think about that. Somewhere in the obedient Christian life, we have to be willing to pour out our lives for others. That's going to mean giving up time and space. It's going to mean giving up comfort and safety. It's going to mean giving up privilege and the respect we think we're owed.

At City Pres, we host concerts in our building. We didn't plant a church and acquire a building in order to host concerts, but when a local musician we know asked whether he could have an event in our space we said we would think about it. The guy (a non-Christian friend) said the songwriters were tired of playing in smoky bars at 1 a.m. with no one listening. In order to practice what we preach about generosity and loving the city, we said yes. This seemed like something we could do to love a group of people who didn't feel loved by the church.

You can disagree with our decision, but it has resulted in a number of people asking questions and even visiting our church, people who don't go to church anywhere else. But even if no one from a concert attends City Pres, it's still a privilege and joy to engage people with the generous, no-strings-attached love of Christ. In a small way, we are pouring out a drink offering to the Lord.

Paul rejoices with the Philippians, and he calls them and us to joy. He writes, *"I am glad and rejoice with you all. Likewise you also should be glad and rejoice with me"* (Phil. 2:17b–18). It's an invitation to something different. Paul had every reason to be cynical, mean, grumbling, and complaining. His life as a Christian had been anything but easy. But his focus was on Jesus. Instead of grumbling, there can be both a general and specific joy in our lives. It's a joy for what God has done in our lives and in the lives of others.

One of the things I haven't mentioned about this passage is that these "yous" are plural, not singular.

They're really "y'alls." We're a together people, not a collection of individuals. We are brought into the family of God with others. We work out our salvation together, in the context of community. We are to be lights pushing back darkness, together. It's not just you with a single flashlight going into a cave, but all of us together illuminating the whole place so it's not dark anymore, and so we're not alone anymore.

There was a Verizon cell phone network commercial where the woman is talking about her plan, and then the camera pans back and you see she has a whole network behind her. It's not just her on the phone; there are thousands of people standing with her as part of her network.

As Christians, we have a network. It may be smaller than we want or weirder than we want, but it will grow bigger as more people see they need this joy, need this light, and need this Gospel message for their lives.

Epaphroditus is a part of that network, our network, and he has the same joy. He almost died helping others. Both Paul and Epaphroditus gave up first place in their lives. They gave up worldly success and embraced suffering for joy. We're being asked to imitate them and imitate Christ who poured himself as a drink offering for us to bring about our salvation and freedom. He loved us. He came to earth from heaven. He gives you his resurrection so you can not fear death but know you will spend eternity with God in heaven.

This obedience, this imitation, and this joyful sacrifice are only possible through the love of Christ. It's only possible if you are living for someone else. It's only possible if your life is so rooted in the divine life of Christ, in his perpetual love and devotion, in *his* death, suffering, and resurrection that nothing will shake you. When you have the confidence of being united to Christ like this, you also have the humility to constantly remember and realize he loves you, not because of you, but because of him.

We get a taste of this when Paul writes about his friend, ". . . *for he nearly died for the work of Christ, risking his life to complete what was lacking in your service to me*" (Phil. 2:30). Why did Epaphroditus nearly die? For the work of Christ. What did Paul say about himself? To live is Christ and to die is gain.

How can we obey the call of Christ on our lives? Not by just pulling ourselves up by our bootstraps and living better. Neither is it by throwing up our hands and saying, "Forget it!"

We must look to Jesus and embrace him in all he is. As Paul said in Philippians 2:4–8:

> *Let each of you look not only to his own interests, but also to the interests of others. Have this mind among yourselves, which is yours in Christ Jesus, who, though he was in the form of God, did not count equality with God a thing to be grasped, but made himself nothing, taking the form of a servant, being born in the likeness of men. And being found in human form, he humbled himself by becoming obedient to the point of death, even death on a cross.*

Look to Jesus. Embrace Jesus. That's why we can sacrifice for others. We don't do it to earn our salvation; we do it because we have that grace already. We work out our salvation because we have it. Jesus gave up everything to come and save you and me. He was and is the drink offering. He is the peace offering. He is the grain offering. He is the Lamb of God who takes away the sins of the world. He gave up all his privilege so we could be found. This is our joy!

You can't just "do better." You have to change who and what you're living for. If you haven't before, repent and believe Jesus loves you and his plans are best for you. Don't just add Jesus to your own plans. Don't just add morality on top of your list. Get down into the core of your being and change. Be changed by Christ. Call out to him for his goodness and mercy in your life!

Jesus didn't just risk his life. He gave it for his people. He came and died for sinners like me and like you. It's not simple or pretty; it's messy. Jesus loved prostitutes and lepers. He opened his life to so much misinterpretation and did things that religious people thought were shocking and completely improper. But that's what made him attractive and approachable to messed up people. That's what still makes him beautiful and believable.

So I sort of scratch my head at this mundane travelogue passage because I want Paul to stay up on the mountaintop of Philippians 2:1–11, talking about Jesus's life, death, and resurrection. But here he is, talking about everyday life. Traveling. Sickness. It just feels so— normal. Normal obedience. Normal lives to imitate. Normal encounters with people who need grace and love. In this chapter, we go straight from amazing theology into boring life. It's almost like we're watching the video of my 12.8 weeks of sleep over the past 284 days. I want to snooze while I watch myself snooze. But how should we think about obedient, sacrificial normal? How can we find joy in everyday life, especially with regard to our sin and frequent lack of progress in sanctification?

Reformed University Fellowship (RUF) campus minister Ben Robertson wrote me a story about his life. One of the women in his home church was remarkable. Her name was Mary Edna Anders. She was crippled by polio as a child, and she used a walker and wore orthopedic shoes all her life. She never married. After a lifetime of atheism, she converted to faith in Jesus in her seventies. She'd never had kids of her own and didn't know how to love people very well. She wanted to learn. So she started by loving the kids in her church. Ben tells about how one time when he was five years old, she asked him where to take her great nephew to lunch, and Ben suggested McDonald's for a Happy Meal. She followed his advice, and the next week at church stopped Ben to thank him for the wonderful suggestion, because her nephew loved it. She starting sending Ben cards on his birthday, or if he scored three or four points in his basketball game and it made the paper, or if he got third place in the science fair. Small things. Detailed things. Normal life things.

When she died, it was standing room only at her funeral. The pastor asked those in attendance, "Raise your hand if you ever got a card from Miss Anders." Every hand in the room went up. Ben says, "She made a huge difference in my life and in hundreds of others through small, simple acts of love."

Imitate Mary Edna Anders! Mary Edna Anders was imitating Jesus, who loved her and saved her and made her his. He came down for her. He sacrificed for her. He showered her with kindness and joy. She just lived out the love she knew from him. He was her joy, and her obedient sacrificial joy gave others joy.

CARDINAL NATION

PHILIPPIANS 3:1–21

But whatever gain I had, I counted as loss for the sake of Christ. Indeed, I count everything as loss because of the surpassing worth of knowing Christ Jesus my Lord. For his sake I have suffered the loss of all things and count them as rubbish, in order that I may gain Christ.
—Philippians 3:7–8

My wife, Jennifer, and I (Bobby) lived in St. Louis from 2003 to 2007 while I studied at Covenant Seminary. During that time, we joined the Cardinal Nation, the group of people around the world who root for the St. Louis Cardinals. We attended and watched so many baseball games. Even today, if a game is on TV, chances are good that we are watching.

As a member of the Cardinal Nation, I learned something about people who identify with the Cards: they are actively involved with their team. They tailgate. They throw parties. They have pep rallies even before the season begins. They read about the team every day in the paper and on blogs. They follow transactions. There is a great deal of joy that comes with being a member of the Cardinal Nation.

Cards fans identify with a rich history of winning. When the countdown to Spring Training is on, talk radio is filled with prognostications, always positive. Because of the impressive legacy of nineteen World Series appearances, eleven World Series wins, and many league and division championships, Cardinals fans look forward to a joyful future year after year. Who wouldn't want to be a part of all that success?!

This expectation of winning informs how Cardinals fans live. They are positive and involved. They watch the games. They wear the gear. There's joy during the season, even when injuries happen, because they expect a better future. This identity influences how they see themselves, what they expect, and how they live.

In Philippians Chapter 3, we see something similar, but much greater. This chapter shows us what it means to be a Christian. It speaks of joy. This joy flows from an identity that rests in Christ and looks forward with confidence to a joyful future because of Jesus's track record—namely, the resurrection. Those who belong to Christ are called citizens of heaven, so the future joy works its way into a joyful present.

We're not all quite this excited about faith in Christ and membership in the church. Often we wonder if there is joy to be had now. We look at our lives and feel discouraged. We wrestle with doubt. We might feel burned out. Maybe we don't believe in anything. As we look at this text, we see that Christianity speaks to these issues. We can have hope. We can have joy—because of Christ. We will see this in three ways: the joyful identity, the joyful future, and the joyful present.

Joyful Identity

This passage begins with a warning for the Philippian church that we should heed as well because it speaks to the essence of Christianity. The warning is to beware the mindset that focuses on what you do to prove your faith, rather than what Christ has done. It is a struggle we all face when we try to justify ourselves by cleaning up, looking good for others, and focusing on ourselves. We are warned that confidence in ourselves saps and destroys joy.

To prove this, Paul provides his credentials. He points to his lineage, especially his religious upbringing. He was a Pharisee of Pharisees, which meant he obtained the holy grail of religious scholarship and zeal in his day. Yet he says those things are meaningless without Christ. Those things are joyless without Christ.

The heart of Christianity is reliance upon Jesus's work and not our own religious pedigree and deeds. That does not mean good deeds don't matter, rather it explains why they matter: because of Christ. They matter because our trust is in Christ alone.

We need Paul's message in America, especially in a widespread church culture, because Christianity is often not associated with joy. The stereotype is dutiful, dreary, pessimistic. It's tiring and exhausting. Many people grow up in church, check off the to-do list, and then leave church during college or soon after. They did the church camp thing, wore the purity ring, listened to the Christian bands, went to youth group and Sunday School, and then left. They were burned out. They never experienced the kind of joy Paul describes in this passage.

Since I grew up in Oklahoma, I can relate to this. Let me give a few examples. In my early twenties, one of my good friends and I were talking about adult life after college. He said to me, "I think I need to be re-baptized." I asked him why he thought that. He said, "Well, in high school and for a few months in college, I just didn't feel Christian. I don't know if I lived up to it. I even made out with a girl once." You see, his conception of his faith was based upon what he did and how he felt, not upon Jesus.

I had another friend who was baptized and then dunked again several other times. Each time was because he exhausted himself so much by following rules and duties and pedigrees that when he broke down, he didn't feel like he was really a Christian. Then he had another awakening, conversion experience and had to make sure this time his baptism was real.

Like my friends, I grew weary from the constant self-examination and failure to live up to the impossible demand of continual piety. In fact, I wanted to walk away from Christianity when I was twenty-three. I was exhausted. There was no joy. Sunday worship felt like a chore. Going to church twice on Sunday and making sure I was there on Wednesday was dreadful. Keeping up appearances, listening to the right music, having the right friends, voting for the right candidate, and believing the right theology wore me out. I nearly left. I was depressed, tired, cynical, and bored, and what I did and heard on Sunday had little impact on my day-to-day life. Really, it was only fear and the shame of disappointing my family that kept me in line.

One Sunday morning, I stumbled into a tiny church in little Minco, Oklahoma, and heard a sermon from Ephesians 5. For those thirty minutes, I was transfixed because the pastor grounded his sermon in the heart of Christianity, the grace of Jesus Christ. Finally, it seemed to make sense. The joy of faith and hope for life were not based on how well I performed, but rather on the work of Christ, in his life, death, and resurrection. Because of

Christ, there was joy to be had in this life! He was perfectly righteous so sinners like me could be counted righteous before God by trusting in him. Jesus sounded beautiful, gracious, and loving.

This message of grace instead of duty and pedigree matters to our hearts. It's something Paul wrote about, and it connects with us today as well. We can fall into the trap of thinking God is pleased with us by what we bring to the table. We start to list our CV and take pride in it. When we focus on those achievements, we miss out on the joy of abiding in Christ.

Paul tells us that because of *Jesus*, God is pleased with us. We don't have to work any harder. We don't have to clean up to approach him. We don't have to check a list. We rest in Christ. Having our identity in Christ means he is for us when we stumble in this world, when we face trouble, when we are ridiculed, and even when we doubt. We can have a joyful identity because of Christ and a joyful future found in him.

Joyful Future

This passage tells us faith in Jesus gives us hope to endure. It gives us the perspective to see our own good deeds as rubbish in comparison to the beauty of Christ. It also gives us the perspective to struggle, deal with pain, suffer, and yet still see something worth living for: the joyful future grounded in resurrection.

Christianity hinges on the truth or falsity of resurrection. If resurrection is true, then we have hope. We look forward to a joyful future. Paul explains to the Philippian church and to those in Christ's church today that his own sufferings, betrayals, trials, and imprisonments are not in vain because he anticipates the goal of human history—resurrection of the body.

Paul says, *"I press on toward the goal for the prize of the upward call of God in Christ Jesus"* (Phil. 3:14). That prize is resurrection. Our prize is resurrection, based on the resurrection of Christ himself. If the resurrection is true, there is a joyful future. The Bible, from beginning to end, is a book that grounds itself in resurrection. Christianity is a faith hinged on resurrection.

The idea of resurrection in Christianity means death is going away. It means we look forward to an existence that does not include death. Death is eradicated. It also means we look forward to a future where our bodies don't break down from age. We look forward to a future of eternal life where we experience the joy of living without the pain and sadness we currently experience time and again.

Christianity gives hope by pointing us to a joyful future. This teaching sets it apart from other religions. Instead of the elimination of this world or the transformation from being a person to a spirit, Christianity teaches that all that is broken down will be renewed and resurrected because Christ defeated death. Christianity teaches that death, sadness, sickness, brokenness, sin, hatred, racism, war, classism, discrimination, fatherlessness, motherlessness, and all the problems we see will go away. They will go away not because this world will be destroyed, but because life will win. Goodness will prevail. Death will be no more. Joy will defeat sadness because Christ is risen. It is this hope for a joyful future that has fueled Christians through the ages.

In February, 2015, the world was shocked at news that came from Libya. On a sandy beach on the Mediterranean Sea, the terrorist group ISIS beheaded twenty-one Christians. Each of these men had a chance to deny his faith. On the released video footage, it is clear one of the men was praying. In April, a similar scene played out with thirty Christians executed by gunfire. Many others have been captured and killed. There was also a story of 150 Christians kidnapped in Syria. Yet in the Middle East, we see Christians persevere.

Why? It is that hope of a joyful future, that hope in the resurrection. It is that hope that fuels endurance because Christ was betrayed. Christ died, defeated death, and rose again. These men, women, and children were able to endure because their joyful identity in Christ prepared them for the joyful future, resurrection.

We do not live in the Middle East. We are not like the apostles who were jailed for their faith. In fact, Christianity still enjoys a privileged place in American culture. I can wear my clergy collar without fear. Our church is still able to host a Bible study at the Oklahoma State Capitol on Wednesdays. We don't encounter the horrors Christians face elsewhere.

But there are other challenges we face as Christians in our culture. Sometimes our privilege can make us lazy, causing us to overlook and ultimately miss out on the hope for the resurrection. Others of us need resurrection hope because we have experienced great evil in our lives or our bodies are breaking down. We might become disillusioned because life is too ordinary, too mundane. We miss the goal. We miss the hope of the joyful future.

Christianity is a faith of hope. Faith in Jesus is a hopeful faith, because it calls its followers to live life in light of a hopeful future. It says we can have joy now because of the work of Christ—past, present, and future. It says we can endure hard times and be joyful because of our eternal perspective. It's not naive optimism, but a grounding in the truth that this life matters, this world matters, and that the evils we see will one day be gone.

We look forward to the joyful future because of Christ.

However, we also acknowledge the call for Christians to bring future reality to our present lives.

Joyful Present

Our hope for the future can be seen in the way we live in the present. The church Paul was writing to in Philippi was essentially a colonial outpost. The idea of a higher citizenship was something the audience would have understood quite well. Philippi was populated with retired Roman soldiers and miners. So when the text says in Philippians 3:20, *"our citizenship is in heaven,"* the original audience could relate from their own experiences. These were Romans who lived somewhere else, but through their Roman-ness, Philippi became a miniature Rome. Paul calls this outpost church to be a colony of heaven on earth.

As people who live in the United States, we understand his point to a degree. When I took graduate-level history seminars on Colonial America and Latin America, I read about the effects of colonialism. A colony is simply an outpost of one nation that finds itself intentionally in another nation. We can debate the good and bad of such colonialism, but it is a way to spread influence and demonstrate a different way of life. The British influence on the United States of America came from their relationship as mother country and colony, respectively. It is why the majority language in Latin America is Spanish. Both British and Spanish cultures fundamentally changed in their new lands. Their citizenship was somewhere else, not indigenous to their physical location.

When this passage tells us "our citizenship is in heaven," it is not telling us to sit idly by on earth, waiting to die or for Christ to return. It's a call to work for a joyful present because of our actual citizenship that resides somewhere else—in heaven. If we believe the resurrection matters for the future, then it should affect our present. Future hope works in the present.

Christianity is not about going to heaven. It is about bringing heaven to earth. Heaven is where the glory of God resides. The Scriptures speak of God's glory dwelling on earth—heaven came to earth in the person of Christ. Christians, as people who are called to imitate Christ, should be involved in bringing about the Kingdom of God on earth. We demonstrate where we belong in the future by how we live today.

Paul is not calling us to pessimism when we see evil. Remember that Rome was full of hundreds of religions and was hostile to Christianity. There was no call to sit back because evil was too great. Nor do we see in Paul's letter to the Philippians a call to naive optimism, where Christians are called to live as though there's nothing wrong with their society. There's a temptation many feel to pull back and get safe, but that's not living as a citizen of heaven. Instead, there is a call to engage with others around us in joy. And in the joy, we live in the tension between the current reality and the reality to come.

What does that mean for us? It means we have work to do! If the resurrection matters, then it affects life. It means our day-to-day interactions have meaning, because we represent the glory that is to come. Our jobs are not mundane. They are a holy calling. Our friendships matter. Our lives matter. We are called to represent God's glory here and make this world a better place.

If we believe there is a future without racism, then we work against racism today. We don't just say, "one day…." If we value the lives of children, we get involved in foster care and adoption. We reach out. We love. If we love our city, we work to make it better. We can do that by joining a school board, teaching a kid to read, volunteering at a nonprofit, giving to people in need, helping others learn job skills, or in many other ways.

Our resurrection hope calls us to be good citizens of heaven by bringing heaven to earth. Our city of Oklahoma City is full of opportunities to serve. So is yours! Christians are called not just to minister in word, but also in deed. That's the idea of being a citizen of heaven and yet living now on earth. It's not a political agenda, it's a people agenda. Our love for God leads us to demonstrate love for others and care for the world around us. We're not called to be against our world but to demonstrate there is a better country, one whose builder and maker is God. We do that today. Our joyful future leads us to live in a joyful present as we care and sacrifice and demonstrate the love of Jesus toward others.

This flows out of our understanding of who we are, our identity in Christ. When we are grounded in who we are in him, we have a joyful identity. As the old hymn by the same name says, "Jesus paid it all." This understanding of God and ourselves provides a joyful future. The Christian hope is resurrection. Death will be no more; behold—all things are becoming new. Because of our hope in resurrection, we work to create a joyful present as our identity informs how we live in this present world. We don't exist for ourselves; we exist to glorify God and for the sake of others.

There is joy because Christ died and rose again. We can have joy today, even in hard times. May God grant that we keep our eyes fixed upon Jesus, the author and completer of our faith.

CARPET JOY

PHILIPPIANS 4:1–23

Rejoice in the Lord always;
again I will say, rejoice.
—Philippians 4:4

My (Bobby's) friend, Chris, was married recently, and I was honored to be a member of the wedding party. Like many weddings, it was not without its logistical issues. In fact, the best man was unable to attend because he was deployed to Iraq, so he had to figure out how to fulfill his duty to the groom long distance.

Friday night, during the reception, the best man gave his speech via downloaded video on a large TV screen. Talk about stealing the show! In his speech, which took nine minutes, he gave Chris and Vicky an important charge, calling them to essential things, despite not being there to tell them in person. He explained the importance of joy that can be found in marriage. He talked about the importance of two people working through disagreements and the joy of friends, family, and having community.

He spoke of the need to see love, and how commitment can provide joy even in hard times. He ended with the need for partnership. He said marriage is not just two people, but two partners, and these partners are not in the marriage alone. They each have a partner who will support them and who they can support. The best man emphasized that marriage was not something Chris and Vicky should try to do alone.

We all clapped and cheered. It was a wonderful message to a new couple. Paul shares a similar message in Philippians 4, which also calls people to joy in partnership. Paul speaks of conflict and the need for a joyful community. He speaks of contentment, and how through Christ we can realize our joyful provision, even in hard times. Paul also speaks of the need for partnership, which shows the far-reaching implications of the Gospel and how Christ's love is for those we may least expect. He knows walking in community can be difficult, but he says it's worth it.

Community can be scary because when we open ourselves to others, conflict inevitably arises. Churches experience conflict all the time, so we get wary of this type of community. American culture is an individualistic society that thrives on the idea of self-sufficiency and going it alone—so who needs more stress and fighting?! We need to see how knowing Christ puts conflict in perspective.

Joyful Community

Philippians Chapter 4 begins with a disruption. Apparently, there was conflict between two prominent women of the Philippian church, Euodia and Syntyche. Paul says these two, along with Clement, labored side by side with him. They were part of the Gospel partnership that helped birth this church. They had been in the trenches, laboring to share the message of Christ. They worked alongside an apostle. They were valuable, known members of this church. And still, there was a disagreement.

Paul calls Euodia and Syntyche to agree on the things that matter, to agree in the Lord. He calls them to focus on the true, the beautiful, and the good. He calls them to see themselves for who they are in Christ and to work from there to get through their conflict.

We, too, deal with disagreement in our churches. Disagreement and conflict can destroy joy when we define people solely by the views they hold in opposition to our own. We do not see in this passage that anyone is called to change her mind, but they are called to agree in the Lord. They are told to focus on the core teachings of Christianity and work from there.

In a local church or denomination, disagreement can ruin the community when we fixate on it. A group of people will never agree on everything. Some of us are Democrats. Some of us are Republicans. Some of us think the sermons are too long; others think they are too short. Some like the songs we sing; some don't like them. Some miss the church being smaller; some wish it were larger. Some like the way we use the building; others don't. And that's OK.

Unity does not mean there is complete agreement on every issue. But the grace of Christ calls us to not interpret people or other churches through the lens of disagreement, because we can do that all day long. We are called to start with what is important or core, which then places disagreements in perspective.

When City Pres purchased and renovated our church building, there were many, many decisions we had to make quickly. We didn't always agree. In fact, the staff had to learn to trust one another and even give up our opinions on some things. There was conflict. Some was good and healthy, and some wasn't helpful.

I probably caused the most conflict. For example, on the day the carpet was installed, I was in Kansas City for our son's adoption hearing. My fellow pastor, Doug, was at Cardinals Spring Training in Florida with his son, Cal. I remember getting a text with the picture of the carpet. I also remember thinking the carpet looked like a bad 80s sweater. Neither Doug nor I had seen the carpet before it was delivered. That might have been a mistake, but we trusted the designer who had picked it out for us. We hadn't wanted to be involved in every detail, and that was one we had given over to the designer.

There was nothing Doug or I could do about the carpet. There were phone calls and texts for the next seventy two hours about the carpet by people who had not seen it in person. There was conflict. Everyone was anxious.

When I returned to town and saw the carpet with the chairs in the right light, I realized how much time I had wasted fretting about it and how small this issue really was in comparison to the mission of our church: to love God, love people, and love the city. The carpet looked fine! I missed out on joy and celebration because I engaged in a silly, ultimately insignificant conflict that seemed incredibly important at the time.

The Christian community should celebrate rather than fight. *"Rejoice in the Lord always; again I will say, rejoice"* (Phil. 4:4). The Christian community is called to *"not be anxious about anything, but in everything by prayer and supplication with thanksgiving let your requests be made known to God"* (Phil. 4:6). The Christian community is called to guard our thoughts. Paul writes, *"Finally, brothers, whatever is true, whatever is honorable, whatever is just, whatever is pure, whatever is lovely, whatever is commendable, if there is any excellence, if there is anything worthy of praise, think about these things"* (Phil. 4:8). Any and all of these commands by Paul would have helped us during our great carpet controversy.

Paul calls us to this different perspective and living. He says, *"What you have learned and received and heard and seen in me—practice these things, and the God of peace will be with you"* (Phil. 4:9).

When we have disagreements within the church, we must focus on the provision of Christ and keep the reality of his love and grace for sinners in mind. This will allow us to have peace in the midst of conflict. When we ally ourselves with the core Gospel truth of Christ, we see that our commonalities outweigh our differences.

It's a rare thing to see agreement in our cynical, twenty-four-hour news cycle world that thrives on anxiety and conflict. What would it look like for people to see churches where the people find joy? What would it look like for a church to have a sense of community where there is joy? We can because of Christ! We can disagree, yet still be unified because of Christ. We can be one. The reason I say this is because Christ not only calls us to be one, but he also empowers us through his Holy Spirit to be one. His grace is greater than our disagreements, differences, and preferences.

When we experience joyful community, it helps us realize there is a joyful provision—Christ.

Joyful Provision

Paul was imprisoned while writing this letter to the Philippian church. He suffered. What was his response? Rejoicing in the hard times because he had received Christ, his joyful provision. Paul says in Philippians 4:10–13:

I rejoiced in the Lord greatly that now at length you have revived your concern for me. You were indeed concerned for me, but you had no opportunity. Not that I am speaking of being in need, for I have learned in whatever situation I am to be content. I know how to be brought low, and I know how to abound. In any and every circumstance, I have learned the secret of facing plenty and hunger, abundance and need. I can do all things through him who strengthens me.

The first source of joy is the care the Philippian church had for Paul and his companions. One reason Paul wrote this letter was to thank them for a financial gift. This church in an outpost city of the Roman Empire took the time to care and show their concern for the Apostle Paul and his companions as they ministered and made their journey to Rome. The Philippian church gave resources for God's mission.

As we think about Paul's words, we have the opportunity to consider whether and how we acknowledge others' giving on our behalf. Do we offer thanks and see the joy when others look out for our benefit? What opportunities are there for us to be generous toward others? How can we show concern and care? Who can we look to in order to find examples and learn so we too can participate in a joyful provision for others?

The second source of Paul's joy is even more important. Paul recounts his suffering and explains his hardships. Yet he says he has enough. He says Christ is the ultimate source of his joy. Christ sustained him in his mission to start new churches and to share the love of Christ no matter what his material conditions were. When Paul says, *"I can do all things through him who strengthens me,"* he's not talking about throwing touchdowns, hitting home runs, or nailing a job interview. He's talking about the ability to endure, for the sake of Christ, because of Christ.

The joy spoken of in Philippians is grounded in Christ. Where is our joy? Too often we base our joy in our aspirations for self-sufficiency. *Entrepreneur Magazine* ran an article titled "Three Steps to Eliminating the Barriers to Becoming Self-Sufficient," where author Terry Powell stated 75 percent of people want to be self-sufficient.[1] We want to be free of others telling us what to do. We want to provide for ourselves. We want the career that will provide us the best material conditions possible. The article says:

Think about your short and long-term goals in terms of ILWE—Income, Lifestyle, Wealth, and Equity. What kind of income would you like to generate, what kind of lifestyle would you like to live, what kind of wealth and equity would you like to build and acquire? This will lay the groundwork on which you can build the next version of you.

This desire to find joy in what we have and own was something the Philippians faced, too. In Roman culture, self-sufficiency was the key to weathering life's storms. In American culture, the same is true. We want to find our joy and happiness in better jobs, better houses, and in what we acquire. We think these things will bring us contentment and happiness. Then we get them and realize the words of *Mad Men*'s troubled protagonist Don Draper are true: "We're flawed because we want so much more. We're ruined because we get these things and wish for what he had."[2]

There's a solution to our problematic quest for self-sufficiency, one that will make us right again. It's Jesus. The Christian message says through Christ we can have the grace to endure this life. Through Christ, we can find joy because we see his life of poverty and hardships was for us, so we could find true life through him. So often we settle and think we can have joy through stuff. Jesus promises us eternal joy through his provision—himself. He gives himself for us and to us and empowers us to endure with joy because the God of the universe promises himself to his children.

This joyful provision then calls us to a joyful partnership to see the message of Christ go throughout the world.

Joyful Partnership

This letter is a partnership letter. It's personal. It includes names of people and cities. It speaks of how Christianity spread throughout the ancient world and to the importance of the joyful partnership that comes through the power of the Gospel.

Embracing Christ puts us in partnership with others. It deepens community. When we see ourselves as part of Christ's mission of redemption and participate within a church, we understand we do not simply live for ourselves. We exist for others. We exist for community. Christianity offers community for the broken and needy. It offers community for all who crave it because we all need it. Community is part of our joyful partnership.

It also means we work together. Paul points to the real partnership he shared with the Philippian church. Paul planted the church. The church prayed for Paul in his missionary efforts. They communicated with him. They sent him money when he needed it. They shared a deep bond with him and gave.

We have the same opportunity. Your church can partner with others, and so can ours. City Pres partners with the Southwest Church Planting Network in our region. They helped us with money and support to get our church started in 2011. We're so grateful. We couldn't have done it without them. So we give to them to partner in planting other churches.

We partner with our denomination for campus ministry and foreign missions. We partner with nonprofits in our city to help in deed ministries. We ask our members and attenders to find where they can partner with us through their time, talents, prayers, and tithes and offerings. We ask them to join a CityGroup (small group) or open their homes to start a new one.

What can you do to partner with people in your church and city? What can you do to join with others in what's already happening or to start something new? When we partner in ministry, we see that the Gospel extends beyond our horizons in our day, just as we see in this letter to the Philippians.

In the beginning of Chapter 4, Paul mentions Euodia and Syntyche and says they labored side by side with him. When Paul wrote this letter, it was inconceivable for women to be held in such regard. Yet Christianity destroys the barriers we create because it says God desires to rescue the world. Where we erect barriers of race and gender and class, God says his redemption is for anyone who believes. It is for the child. It is for women and men and people of every tribe, nation, ethnicity, and language.

It is even for our enemies. The craziest thing about this passage to me is the closing. *"All the saints greet you, especially those of Caesar's household"* (Phil. 4:22). That last phrase shows the extent of Christ's work and the power of a joyful partnership. Caesar was the enemy of the church. Paul was in Caesar's government's custody. He would later be put to death by the Roman Empire. Yet the good news of Jesus Christ was for them also.

The Gospel is for the people we least expect. It is for

our enemies and it is for us. As we partner with others, we learn to lay aside our prejudices and fears. We learn to sacrifice and submit. We see that if the Gospel is for us, then it is for anyone. And we never know how God will use our partnership with others to further his church and kingdom. Christ's redeeming work and the power of his Spirit extend beyond what we can expect, ask, or imagine. Do we believe Christ's love is for our enemies? Do we believe Christ's love can rescue those we might think beyond rescue? If we believe in the power Jesus has to redeem even the worst and most unlikely of sinners, then we must work together to see it happen.

We have seen something similar happen in Oklahoma City. When we started City Pres, Doug and I were hired by a regional body of churches in our denomination called the North Texas Presbytery. They helped with oversight, accountability, and financial support. When we began to meet for worship, we could not have pulled it off without Frontline Church and First Methodist Church, two very different communities from our own. Now that we have our own building, we partner with Midtown Nazarene Church to let them use our space on Sunday evenings. Each of these partnerships has allowed other congregations to multiply, and we see and hear stories of rescue and new faith because of such joyful partnerships.

How well are we doing at joyful partnership? Do we cringe at the thought of "those kinds of people" coming into our building? To some that could refer to homeless people, or immigrants, or concertgoers, or economically struggling people, or those who stumble in because the door is open.

Are we ready to partner with one another to bring all kinds of people into our community? Are we willing to see the joy in partnering with others and making our own sacrifices for the sake of our city, state, nation, and world?

Are we willing to be uncomfortable? I believe that if the Gospel is for the household of Caesar, then it is for anyone.

May we be a joyful community that looks to our joyful provision, Christ, and seeks joyful partnerships so our city, state, nation, and world will see the beauty and grace of Christ and experience the power of his Spirit.

AFTERWORD

This ancient letter to the Philippians gave a new congregation in an out of the way military city a hopeful message of joy. Joy could be found in unity, partnership, suffering, and community as it was grounded in Jesus and his entering into this world to live, die, and rise again. The ancient Church Father Athanasius wrote that we can have hope because Jesus came to this world and overcame what we could not. That is the same message we find in Philippians.

There are many times we struggle to find joy in our lives. We suffer heartache, disappointment, discrimination, conflict, doubt, and fear. Doug and I hope you have seen that, ultimately, true joy is found in something that transcends our experiences. Joy is found in Christ!

Because Jesus came near to us, we are able to be near to him. That changes everything. His grace changes our perspective. We are able to see the world with its problems. We are able to endure our own problems in the world. We can even have joy when life seems difficult. Christ entered in and experienced the rejection we do. Christ entered this world as fully God and fully man so this world could be made whole again. The Christian hope is grounded in the joy that Jesus came to make all things new.

That experience produces joy as we seek to love God and love our neighbor and journey in our own lives. We hope you can better see and experience that joy. May you always find your joy in Christ.

ENDNOTES

Introduction
1. Sheree Johnson, "New Research Sheds Light on Daily
Ad Exposures," SJ Insights, September 29, 2014, //sjin-
sights.net/2014/09/29/new-research-sheds-light-on-
daily-ad-exposures/.

Chapter 1: Double Rainbows All the Way
2. Hungrybear9562, "Yosemitebear Mountain Double
Rainbow 1-8-10," YouTube, 2010,
https://www.youtube.com/watch?v=OQSNhk5ICTI.

3. Dr. Bryan Chappell, "Who's In Charge," Reformed
Youth Ministries, October 12, 2014,
http://rymonline.org/resources/posts/whos-
in-charge-1.

Chapter 4: Everyday, Normal, Mundane Joy
1. "Fascinating Facts About How We Spend the Days of
Our Lives," mirror.co.uk, last modified February 4, 2012,
http://www.mirror.co.uk/news/uk-news/fascinating-
facts-about-how-we-spend-the-days-410973.

Chapter 6: Carpet Joy

1. Terry Powell, "Three Steps to Eliminating the Barriers to Becoming Self-Sufficient," Entrepreneur, February 18, 2015, https://www.entrepreneur.com/article/241890.

2. Lindsay Lowe, "Our 10 Favorite Mad Men Quotes: 'We're Flawed Because We Want So Much More'," Parade, April 10, 2014, http://parade.com/278822/linzlowe/our-10-favorite-mad-men-quotes-were-flawed-because-we-want-so-much-more/.

REFERENCES

Boice, James M. (2006). *Philippians*. Expositional Commentary. Grand Rapids, MI: Baker Books.

Fee, Gordon D. (1995). *Paul's Letter to the Philippians*. New International Commentary on the New Testament. Grand Rapids, MI: Wm. B. Eerdmans.

Johnson, Dennis. (2013). *Philippians*. Reformed Expository Commentary. Phillipsburg, NJ: P & R Publishing.

Lightfoot, J. B. (1994). *Philippians*. Crossway Classic Commentaries. Wheaton, IL: Crossway Books.

Lucado, Max. (2007). *Philippians*. Lucado Life Lessons series. Nashville, TN: Thomas Nelson.

O'Brien, Peter T. (2014). *The Epistle to the Philippians*. New International Greek Testament Commentary. Grand Rapids, MI: Wm. B. Eerdmans.

Wright, N. T. (2010). *Philippians*. N. T. Wright for Everyone Bible Study Guides. Downers Grove, IL: IVP Connect.

ABOUT THE AUTHORS

Doug Serven is a pastor at City Presbyterian Church in Oklahoma City. Doug grew up in southwest Missouri and graduated with a journalism degree from the University of Missouri-Columbia. He worked for The Navigators for four years before going to Covenant Theological Seminary, where he earned an MDiv. Doug then moved to Oklahoma to begin ordained pastoral campus work with Reformed University Fellowship at the University of Oklahoma. He and his wife, Julie, and their four kids moved to Oklahoma City in 2011 to start City Pres.

Doug likes the OU Sooners, the St Louis Cardinals, the OKC Thunder, IPAs, board games, CrossFit, and yoga.

Doug is married to Julie, and they have four children: Ruth, Cal, Drew, and Anna.

Bobby Griffith is a fifth-generation Oklahoman and one of the pastors of City Presbyterian Church in Oklahoma City. After graduating from Covenant Theological Seminary, he finished a master of arts in history and worked in churches in Pennsylvania and Oklahoma. He is working toward his PhD in history at the University of Oklahoma and also teaches History of Christianity at Mid-America Christian University. He and his wife, Jennifer, have one son, Sammy.

Bobby likes the OU Sooners, the St. Louis Cardinals, the OKC Thunder, smoked meats, motorcycles, CrossFit, and... cats.